MadCap Flare 10 De

Scott DeLoach

ClickStart, Inc.
www.clickstart.net

Designer: Patrick Hofmann

Developed in MadCap Flare

ISBN: 978-0-578-13942-5

10

Printed and bound in the United States of America

Dedication

This book is dedicated to my mother, Sylvia Jo DeLoach.
Thanks, mom, for always believing in me.

Contents

Indexes 158

Search 166

Glossaries 172

Format and design 185

Stylesheets 187

Internationalization 339

Flare customization 345

Appendices 353

Additional resources..............................354

Keyboard shortcuts (by task) 355

Keyboard shortcuts (by key) 362

Guide to Flare files 367

Quick task index....................................371

Introduction

This book was designed to be both a study guide for the certified MAD program and a comprehensive guide for Flare users. It meets the needs of a wide range of Flare users, including those who are:

- New to content development, help authoring, and technical writing

- Transitioning from RoboHelp or another help authoring tool

- Transitioning from Word

- Transitioning from FrameMaker

- Upgrading from a previous version

- Looking for a quick 'refresher' of key features

- Preparing to be Certified MAD for Flare™

This book provides the essential information you need to use all of Flare's major features. It also includes information that will appeal to advanced users, such as keyboard shortcuts, Flare file descriptions, and a quick task index.

What is 'Certified MAD for Flare?'

The certified MadCap Advanced Developer (MAD) program recognizes and validates your ability to use MadCap products. Being certified MAD for Flare is the best way to demonstrate your abilities and stay up to date with MadCap Flare. It also sounds cool!

To be certified MAD for Flare, you will need to:

☐ pass the certification test

☐ submit a sample Flare project

About the exam

The certification test is a 75 minute, 50 question test that you take on the Web. The passing score is 70%. The test is not easy—you will need to study and review this book's sample questions to pass. We designed the certification program to be a true assessment of Flare users' advanced abilities, and we want those who pass to be proud to be Certified MAD for Flare!

About the sample project

The sample project is a Flare project that demonstrates your ability to use Flare. The project does not have a time limit, and you can choose the subject.

Preparing for certification

The best way to prepare for the certification test is to take a Flare class. The questions on the test are drawn directly from the course guides and class content. You will also learn best practices for creating Flare projects, which will help you successfully pass the sample project requirements.

This guide is also a great way to prepare for certification, and it is designed to complement the training classes. The questions at the end of each chapter are similar to the test questions, and they can be used to review Flare features before taking the test. The step-by-step instructions will help you successfully create the sample project.

Icons used in this guide

The following icons are used throughout this guide to help you find important and time-saving information.

Icon	Meaning	Description
⚠	Caution	Important advice that could cause data loss or unnecessary aggravation if not followed.
NEW!	New Feature	A new or substantially enhanced feature in Flare 10.
◇	Note	Additional information about a topic.
TIP▶	Tip	A recommended best practice, shortcut, or workaround.

Updates

For the most up-to-date information about this book, see **www.clickstart.net**.

For the most up-to-date information about Flare, see MadCap Software's website at **www.madcapsoftware.com** and the Flare forums at **forums.madcapsoftware.com**.

What's new in Flare 10

Flare 10 includes over 300(!) user-requested enhancements. The major new features are listed in the table below.

To review the list of user-requested enhancements, see kb.madcapsoftware.com/#Flare/General/GEN1041F_-_FlareV10_Release_Notes.htm

Feature	See Page(s)
Enhanced project templates	28
Convert equations in FrameMaker documents to MathML	43, 45
Smart quotes	64
Insert multiple table rows or columns	89
Image maps with condition tag	120
before and after pseudo classes	192
Curved borders	198
Style comments	202
Responsive output for HTML5 targets	228
Multiple variable definitions	236
Date/time variables	237
Eclipse Help	256
Automatically save build log	269
Find and replace widget	290
Built-in support for Perforce	313
Export project	326
Scrollbars for WebHelp when stylesheets are disabled	336
Analyzer search result limits	349
Crash reporting	354

Six reasons to use Flare

Flare is an advanced XML-based content authoring application with powerful single sourcing features. In addition to its innovative user interface and excellent online help, Flare has many strengths that make it a great choice for developing online help, policies and procedures, knowledge bases, user guides, and technical manuals. This section lists six reasons why I use Flare and recommend it to clients.

XML-based architecture and clean code

Flare's XML-based architecture allows MadCap to support multiple XML schemas such as XHTML and DITA and potentially add support for additional schemas such as DocBook in the future. All of Flare's project files are XML-based, so they're extremely small and easy to read in Notepad or an XML editor.

Flare's XML-based authoring also means that it produces clean code.

Content linking

Flare allows you to import content from Microsoft Word, Adobe FrameMaker, HTML, XHTML, and DITA documents and from other Flare projects. When you import content, you can link the imported topics to the source document or Flare project.

Content linking allows you to maintain your content in different applications and reuse it in Flare. For example, anyone within your company can develop content in Word, and you can import their content into your Flare project. If you have multiple Flare projects, you can link common formatting elements such as stylesheets and page layouts and reuse them.

Page layouts

Page layouts can be used to set the page size and margins and to set up headers and footers for print targets. Flare's page layouts are very advanced: you can set up different headers and footers for title, first, empty, odd, and even pages, and you can create and use multiple page layouts. For example, you can use a landscape page layout for wide topics and a two-column page layout for your index.

Snippets

Snippets can be used to reuse any content, including text, images, and tables in multiple topics. You can use snippets to reuse a note, a procedure, or even a screenshot and its description.

Source control support

Because Flare has an open XML architecture, Flare projects are compatible with most source control applications, including Perforce, Subversion (SVN), Visual SourceSafe (VSS), and Team Foundation Server (TFS). Flare provides integrated support for Perforce, VSS, TFS, and SVN, which means you can check files in or out and perform other source control tasks from within Flare. You can even set up Flare to automatically send an email or instant message to another team member if you need to check out a file they have open.

Table styles

In other help authoring tools and HTML editors, you must use inline formatting to format tables. If you need to change the table formatting, it's usually very tedious and time consuming.

In Flare, you can use table styles to specify table borders, background colors, captions, and other properties. You can even format header and footer rows and set up alternating background colors for rows and columns. Flare allows you to create multiple table styles, so you can create online- and print-specific table styles.

Projects

This section covers:

- Creating a new project
- Converting from RoboHelp
- Importing HTML Help files
- Converting from FrameMaker

New projects

Project files have a .flprj extension (for 'Flare project'). Flare's project file is a small XML file—feel free to open it in Notepad and take a look.

The project file is stored in your project's top-level folder. You name this folder when you create a new project. For example, if your project is named 'MyFirstProject,' your top-level folder is named 'MyFirstProject.' By default, Flare creates your top-level folder in the My Documents\My Projects folder.

In addition to the project file, your top-level folder contains four subfolders: Analyzer, Content, Project, and Output.

The **Analyzer** folder contains data for the Analyzer reports, such as broken links and topics that are not in a TOC or index.

The **Content** folder contains all of your topics, images, sounds, stylesheets, and movies.

The **Project** folder contains your conditional tag sets, context-sensitive help map files, glossaries, skins, TOCs, and variable sets. Wondering where the index file is? There's not one—Flare stores your index keywords in your topics.

The **Output** folder contains your generated targets, like HTML Help or print documents.

'Which languages does Flare support?'

Flare provides full support for the following languages:

☐ Arabic	☐ German	☐ Spanish
☐ Danish	☐ Hebrew	☐ Swedish
☐ Dutch	☐ Italian	☐ Thai
☐ English	☐ Norwegian	☐ Urdu

| ☐ Finnish | ☐ Persian | ☐ Yiddish |
| ☐ French | ☐ Portuguese | |

Flare supports Unicode, so you can write your topics in any language. Flare also includes translated WebHelp skins for the languages listed above and for numerous region-specific languages. For more information, see 'Selecting a language for a target' on page 343.

The Flare interface can be viewed in English, French, German, or Japanese. You can change the language in the Select UI Language dialog box when you open Flare. If the dialog box does not appear, you can turn it on by selecting **File > Options** and selecting the **Show Select UI Language Dialog on Startup** option.

Creating a new project NEW!

You can create a new project using a template. In fact, you use templates to create everything in Flare, including topics, stylesheets, glossaries, skins, and variable sets. Project templates are much more powerful in Flare 10. They include sample topics, page layouts, master pages, stylesheets, and other files to give you a head start designing your project. If you have your own design files, you can use the 'Empty' template.

Shortcut	Tool Strip	Ribbon
Alt+F, N	🖼 (Standard toolbar)	File > New Project > New Project

To create a new project:

1 Select **File > New Project > New Project**.
  The Start New Project wizard appears.

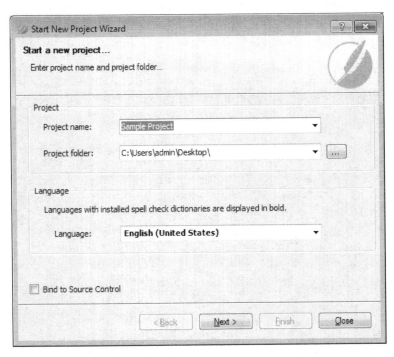

2 Type a **Project Name**.
   You don't have to type the .flprj extension. Flare will add it for you if you leave it out.

3 Type or select a **Project Folder**.

4 Select a **Language** and click **Next**.
   The language you select determines which dictionary is used for spell checking.

5 Select a **Source** and click **Next**.
   You can select a factory template or your own project template. Flare 10 provides many new, professionally designed templates for online and print targets. **NEW!**

6 Select an **Available Target** and click **Finish**.
   Your new project opens in Flare.

Converting from RoboHelp

Flare features that are not in RoboHelp

Flare includes the following features that are not in RoboHelp 11:

Feature	Description	See page(s)
HTML Help import	If you cannot find the source files for an HTML Help (CHM) file, you can import the CHM into Flare.	38
Tag and span bars	Flare displays your tags in the tag and span bars. You can use the tag and span bars to move, sort, or modify content.	59
QR codes	QR codes can provide links to additional information for mobile users.	61
Equations	Flare's Equation Editor can be used to create complex equations.	62
Table styles	Flare provides best-in-class support for formatting tables using table styles.	89
Vector images	Flare supports the SVG, EPS, and PS vector image formats.	99
Toggler links	Toggler links are similar to drop-down links, but they can be used to open or close multiple blocks of content.	128
Relationship links	Relationship links are similar to help controls, but they can be used to group links based on topic types.	135
SEO optimization	SEO ('search engine optimization') features include meta descriptions and site maps.	169 and 261
Redacted style	Redacted content is typically 'blacked' out in confidential documents.	191
WebHelp Mobile format	Flare's WebHelp Mobile target is optimized for viewing on mobile devices such as phones and tablets.	255

Feature	Description	See page(s)
DotNet Help format	DotNet Help is MadCap's help format for .NET applications. Unlike HTML Help, it can run from a file server.	256
DITA and XPS export	Flare can create DITA and XPS targets.	257
FrameMaker export	You can single-source your content by exporting to FrameMaker to create print documents.	264

RoboHelp features that are not in Flare

RoboHelp 11 includes the following features that are not in Flare 10:

Feature	What You Should Do
Automated context-sensitive help authoring	Use Flare's Alias Editor to create context-sensitive help.
Cloud sharing support for Dropbox and SkyDrive	Use a cloud-based source control server such as Google Code.
Content categories	Create multiple online targets.
FlashHelp	Use HTML5 or WebHelp.
Forms	Use another HTML editor to create and edit forms. To open a topic in another HTML editor, right-click the topic and select **Open with** > *your HTML editor*.
JavaHelp	Use DotNet Help, HTML5, or WebHelp.
Oracle Help	Use DotNet Help or WebHelp. If you can't use either of these formats, ask MadCap to add support for Oracle Help. They may add an Oracle Help target type if enough users are interested.
PDF import	Save the PDF document as HTML and import the HTML file.
Scripting	Use keyboard shortcuts and the Quick Access toolbar.

Top ten RoboHelp conversion 'gotchas'

RoboHelp and Flare are similar, but there are some features that are *just* different enough to be confusing. There are also a few Flare features that can be hard to find, especially if you are accustomed to using RoboHelp.

Here's my list of the top ten features that I had trouble understanding, finding, and remembering how to use when I started using Flare.

10 Using the ribbon

By default, Flare uses a more modern ribbon-based UI instead of a toolbar like RoboHelp. If you prefer the toolbar, select File > Options, select the Interface tab, and select Tool Strip.

9 Using condition tag boxes

Flare's Content Explorer provides condition tag boxes to identify topics that use condition tags. Unfortunately, an empty condition tag box looks like a checkbox. I tried to select these boxes for a few days and thought they must be broken. According to the Flare help community, many other users assume they are checkboxes too.

8 Indexing

Indexing is very different in Flare than in RoboHelp. Although Flare does not include an indexing wizard, you can create an 'auto-index phrase set' to automatically add keywords to your topics and an 'index link set' to create 'see also' index entries.

7 Auto-generating a TOC

In RoboHelp, you can auto-generate a TOC based on your Project Manager tab. Folders on the Project tab become books, and topics become pages. If you change the organization on the Project tab, you have to regenerate the TOC or update it yourself.

In Flare, you can auto-generate a TOC book to automatically create links to headings inside a topic. If you add or remove headings in the topic, the TOC is automatically updated.

6 Using templates

In RoboHelp 7 and earlier, a template is used to format topics and include boilerplate content, such as a logo or a header and footer. The headers and footers are dynamically linked to topics. If you change a template's header or footer, topics that use the template are automatically updated.

In Flare, everything (including stylesheets, snippets, tables, topics, and TOCs), uses a template. You can use a template to include boilerplate content and formatting, but it is not dynamically linked to the item you created. If you update a template, the items you created using the template are not updated. However, Flare's master pages *do* allow you to dynamically update topics.

5 Using master pages

In RoboHelp 8, templates were renamed master pages. RoboHelp 8's master pages are similar to Flare's master pages, but Flare's master pages provide more features.

4 Using page layouts

Flare's page layouts can be used to set the page size, page margins, headers and footers for print documents. RoboHelp automatically sets most of these options, but you cannot change them.

3 Viewing RoboHelp's WebHelp vs Flare's WebHelp

RoboHelp's WebHelp and Flare's WebHelp have very different default designs (see page 257 to compare screenshots).

2 Viewing browse sequences

In RoboHelp, browse sequences appear as either a graphical bar at the top of your topics (HTML Help) or as small arrows in the navigation pane (WebHelp). RoboHelp's HTML Help browse sequences require the HHActiveX.dll file to be installed on the user's computer.

In Flare, browse sequences appear as either a TOC item (HTML Help) or as an accordion item (DotNet Help, HTML5, and WebHelp). Because they do not appear on a custom tab, Flare's HTML Help browse sequences do not require a .dll file.

You can add browse sequence next and previous buttons to your WebHelp toolbar using the Skin Editor. For more information, see 'Using a browse sequence' on page 181.

1 Context-sensitive help paths

Flare organizes your generated WebHelp topics in a 'Content' folder. Since RoboHelp does not use a Content folder, your context-sensitive help links might not work after you convert to Flare. If you cannot change the code to include the Content folder, you can remove it from your WebHelp files by selecting 'Do not use 'Content' folder in output' on the Advanced tab in your WebHelp target.

Importing a RoboHelp project

You can import projects created with RoboHelp X5 or later (.xpj files) or RoboHelp X4 or earlier (.mpj files) If you want to import an HTML Help project created with another help authoring tool, see 'Importing an HTML Help file' on page 38.

Shortcut	Tool Strip	Ribbon
none	File > Import Project > RoboHelp Project	File > New Project > RoboHelp Project

To import a RoboHelp project:

1 Select **File** > **New Project** > **RoboHelp Project**.
The Open File dialog box appears.

2 Locate and select a project file.

☐ RoboHelp X5 or later: .xpj file

☐ RoboHelp X4 or earlier: .mpj file

☐ Other tools: .hhp file

3 Click **Open**.
The Import Project Wizard appears.

4 Click **Next**.

5 Type a **Project Name.**

6 Type or select a **Project Folder** and click **Next.**

7 Select whether you want to **Convert all topics at once.**
This option converts your topic files from HTML to XHTML. If you don't select this option, your files will remain as HTML files and your index terms will not be imported.

8 Select whether you want to **Convert inline formatting to CSS styles.**

⚠ *Be careful with this option. If you use a lot of inline formatting, you could end up with hundreds of styles.*

9 Click **Next.**

10 Select a **Language** for spell checking and click **Finish.**
The RoboHelp project is imported into Flare. Your new Flare project file will have a .flprj extension.

'What happens to my... ?'

The following table explains how RoboHelp's features convert to Flare.

RoboHelp Feature	Converts?	Comments
Browse sequences	✓	
Conditional tags	✓	Stored in a condition tag set named 'Primary.'
Custom colors		You must recreate the colors in Flare.
Dictionaries		See 'Where's my dictionary?' on page 36.
HTML topics	✓	Converted to XHTML either when imported (recommended) or when opened.
Folders	✓	
Forms	✓	Forms are converted, but you can only edit them in the Text Editor.
Frames	✓	Frames are converted, but you can only edit them in the Text Editor.

RoboHelp Feature	Converts?	Comments
Glossary	✓	
Inline formatting	✓	Maintained, or you can converted them to styles.
Publishing locations	✓	Converted to 'Publishing destinations.'
Single-Source layouts	✓	Converted to 'Targets.'
Skins		See 'Where are my skins?' on page 37.
Snippets	✓	
Sounds	✓	
Table of contents	✓	
Template headers and footers	✓	Converted to snippets.
Movies	✓	
Variables	✓	Stored in a variable set named 'Primary.'
Windows	✓	Converted to skins.

'Where is my dictionary?' TIP▷

RoboHelp dictionaries are not imported, but you *can* add your dictionary terms to Flare.

To add your dictionary terms in Flare:

1 In Windows Explorer, open the C:\Program Files (x86)\MadCap Software\MadCap Flare V10\Flare.app\Resources\SSCE folder.

2 Find your dictionary.
Dictionary file names are based on their language. For example, Flare's 'English - American' dictionary is named 'ssceam.tlx.'

3 Just to be safe, make a backup copy of your Flare dictionary.

4 Locate your RoboHelp dictionary.
To find your dictionary:

- ☐ Open RoboHelp HTML.

- ☐ Select **Tools** > **Spelling Options**.

- ☐ Select the **Dictionary** tab. Your 'dictionaries' paths are listed in the Path column.

5 Open your RoboHelp dictionary in Notepad.

6 Copy all of your terms and close your RoboHelp dictionary.

7 Open your Flare dictionary in Notepad.

8 Paste your terms at the end of the file.

9 Save your new Flare dictionary.

'Where are my skins?'

RoboHelp skins are imported into Flare, but they are not set up. You can use Flare's Skin Editor to set up your skins.

Importing HTML Help files

You can import an HTML Help .hhp project file or a compiled HTML Help .chm file. If you have the source files and the .hhp file, they will import better. If not, Flare can recreate the source files by decompiling the .chm file.

Creating a new project based on an HTML Help file

You can create a new project based on an HTML Help CHM or HHP file. If you have a CHM file and the source HHP file, you should import the HHP file.

If you want to import a RoboHelp project, see 'Importing a RoboHelp project' on page 34.

Shortcut	Tool Strip	Ribbon
none	File > Import Project > HTML File Set	File > New Project > HTML File Set

To create a new project based on an HTML Help file:

1   To import an HTML Help project file, select **File** > **New Project** > **HTML Help Project (HHP)**.
    To import an HTML Help file, select **File** > **New Project** > **HTML Help File (CHM)**.
    The Open File dialog box appears.

2   Locate and select an HHP or CHM file.

3   Click **Open**.
    The Import Project Wizard appears.

4   Click **Next**.

5   Type a **Project Name**.

6 Type or select a **Project Folder** and click **Next**.

7 Select whether you want to **Convert all topics at once**.
This option converts your topic files from HTML to XHTML. If
you don't select this option, your files will remain as HTML files
and your index terms will not be imported.

8 Select whether you want to **Convert inline formatting to CSS
styles**.
⚠ *Be careful with this option. If you use a lot of inline
formatting, you could end up with hundreds of styles.*

9 Click Next.

10 Select a **Language** for spell checking and click **Finish**.
The HTML Help project is imported into Flare.

Converting from FrameMaker

Top ten FrameMaker conversion 'gotchas'

Flare and FrameMaker have very different interfaces. However, both applications can be used to create print documents. When FrameMaker is combined with Quadralay's WebWorks ePublisher, you can use it or Flare to create online formats such as HTML Help.

If you focus on tasks and features, FrameMaker and Flare are similar applications. It takes time to learn the Flare interface when you transition, just as it takes time to learn FrameMaker. I've created a list of the top ten differences between FrameMaker and Flare to hopefully make the transition easier for you.

10 Keyboard shortcuts

Like FrameMaker, Flare provides extensive keyboard shortcuts (see page 355 for a list). However, Flare uses 'Alt' key shortcuts rather than 'Esc' key shortcuts.

9 Importing content

You can import content into a FrameMaker document, or you can copy and paste content into FrameMaker. In Flare, you can import documents into your project to create new topics. If you want to import content into a topic, you can copy and paste.

8 Inserting graphics

In FrameMaker, images are placed inside anchored or unanchored frames. Placing an image in an anchored frame allows the image to 'move' with the surrounding text. Placing an image inside an unanchored frame fixes its position on the page.

In Flare, images automatically 'move' with the surrounding text. If you place an image inside a div tag, you can fix its position.

7 Cross references and hyperlinks

If you import a FrameMaker document that contains cross references, the cross references convert to Flare cross references. In Flare, you can use hyperlinks or cross references to link to other topics. You can keep using cross references to link to topics, but you will need to use hyperlinks to link to websites or other files like PDF documents.

6 Master pages

In FrameMaker, a master page is used to specify the page layout. In Flare, a master page is used to add content to topics in online targets. For example, a Flare master page can be used to add a copyright statement to the bottom of every topic in HTML Help.

5 Templates and page layouts

A FrameMaker template contains master pages that specify the formatting, header, and footer for different types of pages (for example, title, odd, and even pages). In Flare, a page layout contains pages that are used to format different types of pages.

4 Lists

In FrameMaker, bulleted and numbered lists are paragraph styles. When you import a FrameMaker document, these list styles remain paragraph styles, just like in FrameMaker. In Flare, lists can also be created using the ul ('unordered' or bulleted) list and ol ('ordered' or numbered) list tags rather than the paragraph tag. You can create lists using either method, but it might be confusing to use both approaches in the same project.

3 'Missing' .book files?

Flare does not use .book files. When you import a FrameMaker .book file, Flare will import all of the included .fm files and create a table of contents (TOC) based on your FrameMaker 'TOC' file.

2 Styles

Flare uses styles to format your content. Styles are stored in stylesheets and are basically a combination of the paragraph and character designers in FrameMaker. When you import a FrameMaker document, Flare can create a stylesheet that includes all of your FrameMaker character and paragraph styles. Table styles can also be converted into table-specific stylesheets.

1 Topic-based authoring

In Flare, your content is separated into short (usually 1-4 printed pages) topics rather than long chapter or section documents. It seems weird and unnecessary at first—why do you need so many small topics? The reason small topics are useful is the same reason multiple chapter documents are useful: it's easier to work with focused 'chunks' of content.

In Flare, topics are organized into folders in the Content Explorer and books in the table of contents (TOC). The folders and books are similar to your chapters, and the TOC itself is similar to a FrameMaker .book file. You can easily move topics around in a TOC book, just as you can move .fm chapter documents in a FrameMaker book. You can also easily add new topics to a TOC book. Topic-based authoring also makes it very easy to reuse content in multiple topics. For example, you can reuse a 'Copyright' or 'Conventions in this guide' topic in multiple Flare projects.

Importing a FrameMaker document

When you import a FrameMaker document, you can divide the document into smaller topics based on styles that are used in your FrameMaker document. For example, you can create a new topic for each 'Heading 1' in the document.

Flare can create a stylesheet (.css file) based on the formatting in your FrameMaker document. Or, you can apply an existing stylesheet to reformat your imported topics to match your other topics.

Creating a new project based on a FrameMaker document

You can create a new project based on a FrameMaker document. If you want to import a FrameMaker document into an existing project, see 'Importing a FrameMaker document' on page 45.

◇ *When you import a FrameMaker document, Flare saves your settings in a FrameMaker Import File (these files have a .flimpfm extension). You can reuse these settings when you re-import the FrameMaker document or import similar documents.*

Shortcut	Tool Strip	Ribbon
none	File > Import Project > FrameMaker Documents	File > New Project > FrameMaker Documents

To create a new project based on a FrameMaker document:

1   Select **File** > **New Project** > **FrameMaker Documents**.
    The Import FrameMaker wizard appears.

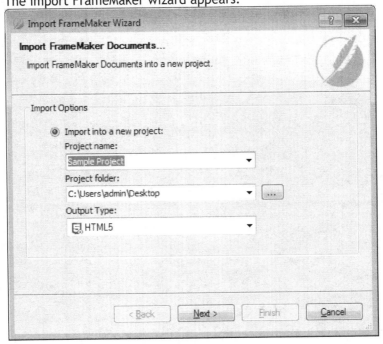

2 Type a **Project Name.**

3 Type or select a **Project Folder.**

4 Select an **Output Type.**
You can add additional output types to your project later.

5 Click **Next.**

6 Click .

7 Select a .fm or .book FrameMaker file and click **Open.**
If needed, you can select more than one FrameMaker document.

8 If you plan to continue editing the file in FrameMaker, select **Link generated files to source files.**

This option allows you to link the imported topics to the FrameMaker document. When you re-import the document, Flare will replace the original topics with the new topics.

Linked topics have a chain (⅋) icon after their file name when opened in the XML Editor.

9 Select a style or styles to use to create new topics.
For example, you can create a new topic for each Heading 1 in the FrameMaker document.

10 Click **Next.**

11 If your images have callouts, select **Generate Images with Callouts.**
This option will create a MadCap Capture "props" file for the callouts, and you can edit the image and callouts in Capture.

12 If you have sized your images in FrameMaker, select **Preserve Image Size.**

13 If you want to automatically reimport the FrameMaker document(s) when you create a target, select **Auto-reimport before 'Generate Output.'**

14 If your document contains equations, select **Convert equations to MathML.** **NEW!**

15 Click **Next.**

16 Select a stylesheet for the new topic(s).
If you select a stylesheet, Flare will apply the stylesheet to your topics and automatically 'map' styles with matching names. If you do not select a stylesheet, Flare will create a stylesheet based on the formatting in your FrameMaker document.

17 Click **Next.**

18 Map (or 'match') your heading-level styles to the h1-h6 heading styles.
For example, if you use a first-level heading style named 'HeadText1' in FrameMaker, map it to 'h1.' Styles will map to the 'p' (paragraph) style by default.

19 Click **Next.**

20 If needed, map your character-level styles, like bold, to Flare styles.
Character-level styles will map to the 'span' tag by default.

21 Click **Next.**

22 If needed, map your cross-reference (x-ref) styles to Flare styles.
Cross reference-styles will map to the MadCap|xref style by default.

23 Click **Finish.**

24 Click **Accept.**

Importing a FrameMaker document into a project

You can import a FrameMaker document into an existing Flare project and divide it into multiple topics.

Shortcut	Tool Strip	Ribbon
Alt+P, I, F	Project > Import File > Add FrameMaker Import File	File > New

To import a FrameMaker document:

1   Select **File** > **New**.
    —OR—
    Right-click the **Imports** folder and select **Add FrameMaker Import File**.
    The Add File dialog box appears.

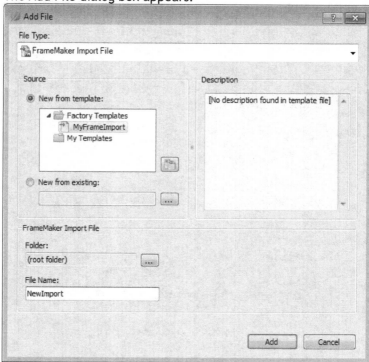

2   For **File Type**, select **FrameMaker Import File**.

3   Select a **Source** template.

4   Type a **File Name**.

5   Click **Add**.
    The Frame Import Editor appears.

6 Click ⊞.

The Open dialog box appears.

7 Select a .fm or .book FrameMaker document and click **Open**.
If needed, you can select more than one FrameMaker
document.

8 If you plan to continue editing the file in FrameMaker, select
Link generated files to source files.

✎ *This option allows you to link the imported topics to the
FrameMaker document. When you re-import the document,
Flare will replace the original topics with the new topics.*

*Linked topics have a chain (⚭) icon after their file name
when opened in the XML Editor.*

9 Select the **New Topic Styles** tab.

10 Select a style or styles to use to create new topics.
For example, you can create a new topic for each Heading 1 in
the FrameMaker document.

11 Select the **Options** tab.

12 If your images have callouts, select **Generate Images with
Callouts**.
This option will create a MadCap Capture "props" file for the
callouts, and you can edit the image and callouts in Capture.

13 If you have sized your images in FrameMaker, select **Preserve
Image Size**.

14 If you want to automatically reimport the FrameMaker
document(s) when you create a target, select **Auto-reimport
before 'Generate Output.'**

15 If your document contains equations, select **Convert equations
to MathML**. **NEW!**

16 Select the **Stylesheet** tab.

17 Select a stylesheet for the new topic(s).
If you select a stylesheet, Flare will apply the stylesheet to

your topics and automatically 'map' styles with matching names. If you do not select a stylesheet, Flare will create a stylesheet based on the formatting in your FrameMaker document.

18 Select the **Paragraph Styles** tab.

19 Map (or 'match') your Word heading-level styles to the h1-h6 heading styles.
For example, if you use a first-level heading style named 'HeadText1' in FrameMaker, map it to 'h1.' Styles will map to the 'p' (paragraph) style by default.

20 Select the **Character Styles** tab.

21 If needed, map your FrameMaker character styles to Flare styles.
Character-level styles will map to the 'span' tag by default.

22 Select the **Cross-Reference Styles** tab.

23 If needed, map your FrameMaker cross-reference (x-ref) styles to Flare styles.
Cross reference-styles will map to the MadCap|xref style by default.

24 Click **Import** in the toolbar.
The Accept Imported Documents dialog box appears.

25 Click **Accept**.
The imported topic or topics appear in the Content Explorer in a folder named after the FrameMaker import file you used.

'What happens to my... ?'

The following table explains how FrameMaker's features convert to Flare.

FrameMaker Feature	Converts?	Comments
Character styles	✓	Added to a stylesheet. By default, they are associated with the span style tag.

FrameMaker Feature	Converts?	Comments
Conditional Tags	✓	Stored in a condition tag set that is named based on your import file.
Cross reference styles	✓	Added to a stylesheet and associated with the MadCap|xref style tag.
Equations	✓	Converted to MathML or images. **NEW!**
Images	✓	Added to a folder in the Content Explorer named after your import file.
Index keywords	✓	Maintained and appear with a green background in your topics. You can hide them if needed.
Inline formatting	✓	Maintained. Can also be converted to styles.
Master pages		You will need to recreate your master page as a page layout in Flare.
Named destinations	✓	Maintained in topics.
Paragraph styles	✓	Added to a stylesheet. By default, they are associated with the p (paragraph) style tag.
Table styles	✓	Converted to table stylesheets.
'TOC' document	✓	Converted to a Flare TOC named after your import file.
Variables	✓	Added to a variable set that is named after your import file.

Sample questions for this section

1 A Flare project file has the following extension:
A) .prj
B) .hhp
C) .htm
D) .flprj

2 Does Flare support Unicode?
A) Yes
B) No

3 Which of the following files can be created based on a template?
A) Topics
B) Stylesheets
C) Snippets
D) All of the above

4 Why should you select 'Link generated files to source files?'
A) To automatically re-import your Word or FrameMaker documents when you build a target.
B) To keep editing your content in Word or FrameMaker.
C) To import your links and cross references.
D) To import images.

5 Which of the following features is imported from RoboHelp but is not set up?
A) Index
B) TOC
C) Variables
D) Skins

6 Can you import FrameMaker .fm files and .book files into Flare?
A) Yes
B) No

7 Which of the following FrameMaker features cannot be imported?

A) Styles

B) Index keywords

C) Master pages

D) All of them can be imported

Topics

This section covers:

- Special characters
- QR codes
- MathML equations
- Smart quotes **NEW!**
- Importing Word, FrameMaker, DITA, and HTML documents
- External resources
- Project linking
- Lists
- Tables
- Images
- Multimedia

Creating topics

In Flare, your content is stored in topics. Each topic is a short (usually 1-4 printed pages) XHTML file that can contain formatted text, images, tables, lists, links, variables, snippets, and other types of content.

'What is XHTML?'

XHTML is a type (or 'schema') of XML. XHTML files use HTML tags, but the tagging conforms to the strict rules of XML. For example, HTML does not require end tags for the <br>, <li>, or <img> tags. In XHTML, all tags must have end tags. So, a break is written in XHTML as <br />. Another difference is that HTML allows upper, lower, or mixed case tags: <BR>, <br>, or <Br>. In XHTML, you must use lowercase tags.

'Do I have to know XML to use Flare?'

Flare has a built-in WYSIWYG ('what-you-see-is-what-you-get') editor called the 'XML Editor.' You don't have to know anything about HTML, XHTML, or XML to use the XML Editor: Flare writes the code for you. If you *do* know how to write XHTML code, you can view the code and change it yourself.

Creating a topic

You can have as many topics in a project as you need. In fact, some Flare projects have over 10,000 topics.

Shortcut	Tool Strip	Ribbon
Ctrl+T	(Content Explorer)	File > New

To create a topic:

1 Select **File** > **New**.
   —OR—
   Click 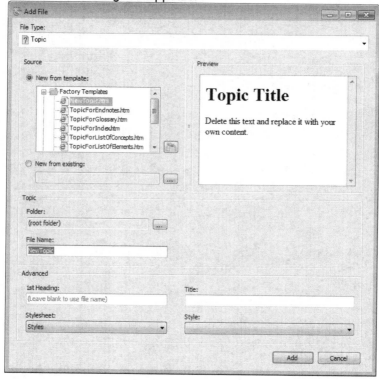 in the Content Explorer toolbar.
   The Add File dialog box appears.

2 For **File Type**, select **Topic**.

3 Select a **Source** template.

4 Select a **Folder** to contain the new topic.

5 Type a **File Name** for the topic.
   You don't have to type the .htm extension. Flare will add it for you don't include it.

6 Click **Add**.
   The topic appears in the Content Explorer and opens in the XML Editor. The Copy to Project dialog box appears.

Viewing your topic titles

In Flare, your topics are listed by their filename in the Content Explorer. However, your users will view your topics by their topic titles in the index and search. Topic titles are also often used in link labels and in the TOC.

By default, your topic titles are automatically set to match the first heading in your topics. You can view and change your topic titles using the File List.

To view your topic titles:

1 Select **View** > **File List**.

2 Scroll to the right to the **Title** column.

📖 *You can click the Title column's heading and drag it to the left to make it easier to find.*

Opening a topic

Topics appear in the Content Explorer. When you double-click a topic, it opens as a new tab in the XML Editor. You can open as many topics as you need.

Shortcut	Tool Strip and Ribbon
Enter	📄 (Content Explorer toolbar)

To open a topic:

1 Select a topic in the Content Explorer.

2 Press **Enter**.
  —OR—
  Click 📄 in the Content Explorer toolbar.
  The topic appears as a new tab in the XML Editor.

Opening a topic in the Text Editor

You can open a topic in the Text Editor to view and edit the XHTML code.

To open a topic in the Text Editor:

1 Open a topic.

2 Click the Text Editor tab at the bottom of the XML Editor window.

TIP *If you click the Auto Complete button, Flare can automatically close your XHTML tags.*

Opening a topic in another editor TIP

You can also open topics in other XHTML editors—if you know where to look!

To open a topic in another HTML editor:

1 Open the Content Explorer.

2 Right-click a topic and select **Open With** > *your XHTML editor*. The topic opens in the HTML editor you selected.

Opening two topics side by side

You can open multiple topics and switch between their tabs, or you can open two topics side by side to compare their content.

To open two topics side by side:

1 Open a topic.
The topic opens as a new tab in the XML Editor.

2 Open another topic.
The second topic opens as a new tab in the XML Editor.

3   Select **Window** > **Float**.
    The selected topic appears in a small floating window.

4   Click the floating window's title bar and drag the window.
    The positioning arrow appears.

5   Drag the window on top of one of the positioning squares.

6   Release your mouse button.

TIP *To move the window back to a tab, select* **Window** > **Float***,
and drag the window to the center positioning square.*

Rearranging open topic tabs

You can rearrange open topic tabs to make it easier to switch between topics.

To rearrange open topic tabs:

1   Open two or more topics.

2 Click an open topic's tab and drag it left or right.

3 Release the mouse button.

The topic's tab will move to its new location.

Using structure bars in a topic

In Flare, you can use the tag and span structure bars to view the tagging behind your topics. The tag bar appears on the left side of the XML Editor, and the span bar appears on the top.

Icon	Description
⧉	Show/hide tag bar
⧉	Show/hide span bar

Inserting a special character

You can insert special characters into your topics, such as ®, ™, ©, non-breaking spaces, and non-breaking hyphens. Common characters are available in the list when you select **Insert** > **Character** or click the ⓐ button in the toolbar. You can also add favorite characters to the list or set the quick character (inserted when you press **F11**).

Shortcut	Tool Strip	Ribbon
F11	ⓐ (XML Editor)	Insert > Character

To insert a special character:

1 Open a topic.

2 Position your cursor where you want to insert the special character.

3 Click the ⓐ button's down arrow.

4 Select a character.

To add a special character to the favorites group:

1 Select **Insert** > **Character**.
The Character dialog box appears.

2 Select a character.

3 Click ⊞.

4 Click **Close**.

To set the quick character:

1 Select **Insert** > **Character**.
The Character dialog box appears.

2 Select a character.

3 Click ⊞.

4 Click **Close**.

Inserting a QR code

A QR code is a type of barcode that can be read by a smart phone application. You can insert a QR code to display additional information, open a website, or send an email.

Shortcut	Tool Strip and Ribbon
Ctrl+Q	Insert > QR Code

To insert a QR code:

1 Open a topic.

2 Position your cursor where you want to insert the QR code.

3 Select **Insert** > **QR Code**.
The Insert QR Code dialog box appears.

4 On the General tab, select a **Content Type**.

5 Type the **Content**.

6 Select a **Size**.

7 Type an **Alternate Text** description of the QR code.
For example, 'QR code link to www.mywebsite.com.' Alt text
is recommended by Section 508 of the U.S Government's
Rehabilitation Act and the W3C's Web Content Accessibility
Guidelines (WCAG).

8 Click **OK**.

Inserting an equation

You can use Flare's Equation Editor to insert equations into a topic.

◇ *If you insert an equation into a heading, the equation will not
appear in cross reference link text or in your table of contents.*

Shortcut	Tool Strip and Ribbon
Ctrl+E	Insert > Equation

To insert an equation:

1 Open a topic.

2 Position your cursor where you want to insert the equation.

3 Select **Insert** > **Equation**.
The Equation Editor appears.

4 Use the ribbons and toolbars to create the equation.

5 Type an **Alternate Text** description of the equation.
For example, alt text for 'e=mc2' would be 'E equals m c squared.' Alt text is recommended by Section 508 of the U.S Government's Rehabilitation Act and the W3C's Web Content Accessibility Guidelines (WCAG).

6 Click **OK**.

Using smart quotes 🆕

You can use smart (i.e. "curly") quotes instead of straight quotes in your topics.

Shortcut	Tool Strip	Ribbon
Alt+F, T	Tools > Options	File > Options

To use smart quotes:

1 Select **File** > **Options**.
The Options dialog box appears.

2 Select the **XML Editor** tab.

3 Select **Replace straight quotes with smart quotes**.

4 Click **OK**.

Finding an open topic

If Flare does not have enough room to display each topic's tab, the additional topics appear in a drop-down list.

To find an open topic in the XML Editor:

1 Click the ☰ down arrow on the right side of the XML Editor.

2 Select a topic in the drop-down list.

Closing all open topics

When you start using Flare, you will probably forget to close topics. If you have too many topics open, you can close all of them at once.

To close all open topics:

☐ Select **Window** > **Close All Documents**.
All of the open documents close.

To close all open topics except the current topic:

☐ Select **Window > Close All Documents Except This One.**
All of the open documents close except the current
document.

Deleting a topic

When you delete a topic, Flare moves the topic to the Windows recycle
bin. If you need to temporarily remove a topic from your project, you
can assign a condition tag to the topic and exclude it from your targets.
For more information, see 'Applying a tag to content in a topic' on
page 245.

Shortcut	Tool Strip	Ribbon
Delete	✖ (Standard toolbar)	Home > Delete

To delete a topic:

1 Select the topic in the Content Explorer or File List.

2 Press **Delete.**
The Delete confirmation dialog box appears.

3 Click **OK.**

4 If anything links to the topic, the Link Update dialog box
appears.

5 Click **Remove Links.**
The topic is moved to the recycle bin.

Importing Word documents

When you import a Word document, you can divide the document into smaller topics based on styles that are used in your Word document. For example, you can create a new topic for each 'Heading 1' in the document.

Flare can convert your Word template (.dot or .dotx file) into a stylesheet (.css file) so your formatting stays the same. Or, you can apply an existing stylesheet to reformat your imported topics to match your other topics.

 Flare requires Word 2003 or later to import .doc files.

Creating a new project based on a Word document

You can create a new project based on a Word document. If you want to import a Word document into an existing project, see 'Importing a Word document' on page 69.

 When you import a Word document, Flare saves your settings in an MS Word Import File (these files have a .flimp extension). You can reuse the import file when you re-import the Word document, or you can use it to import similar documents.

Shortcut	Tool Strip	Ribbon
none	File > Import Project > MS Word Documents	File > New Project > MS Word Documents

To create a new project based on a Word document:

1 Select **File** > **New Project** > **MS Word Documents**.
   The Import Microsoft Word wizard appears.

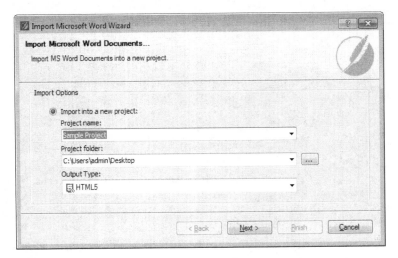

2   Type a **Project Name**.

3   Type or select a **Project Folder**.

4   Select an **Output Type**.
    You can add additional output types to your project later.

5   Click **Next**.

6   Click ⊞.

7   Select a Word document and click **Open**.
    If needed, you can select more than one Word document.

8   If you plan to continue editing the file in Word, select **Link generated files to source files**.

    This option allows you to link the imported topics to the Word document. When you re-import the document, Flare will replace the original topics with the new topics.

    Linked topics have a chain (⧉) icon after their file name when opened in the XML Editor.

9   Click **Next**.

10 Select a style or styles to use to create new topics.
    For example, you can create a new topic for each Heading 1 in the Word document.

TIP▶ *Flare will automatically create new topics based on manual page breaks in your Word document. You may want to remove manual page breaks before importing.*

11 Click **Next**.

12 Select whether you want to create new topics based on the length of your Word document. If you decide to create new topics, you can also automatically add links to the previous and next topics.

13 If your Word document uses different headers and/or footers for different sections, select **Create a Page Layout for each section header/footer**.

14 Click **Next**.

15 Select a stylesheet for the new topic(s).
If you select a stylesheet, Flare will apply the stylesheet to your topics and automatically 'map' styles with matching names. If you do not select a stylesheet, Flare will create a stylesheet based on the formatting in your Word document.

16 Click **Next**.

17 Map (or 'match') your Word paragraph-level styles to your stylesheet's (.css) styles.
For example, if you use a style named 'HeadText1' in Word, map it to 'h1.' Styles will map to the 'p' (paragraph) style by default.

18 Click **Next**.

19 Map any character-level styles, like bold, to your stylesheet's styles.
Character-level styles will map to the 'span' tag by default.

20 Click **Finish**.

Importing a Word document

You can import a Word document into an existing Flare project and divide it into multiple topics.

Shortcut	Tool Strip	Ribbon
Alt+P, I, W	Project > Import File > Add MS Word Import File	File > New

To import a Word document:

1 Select **File** > **New**.
  —OR—
  Right-click the **Imports** folder and select **Add MS Word Import File**.
  The Add File dialog box appears.

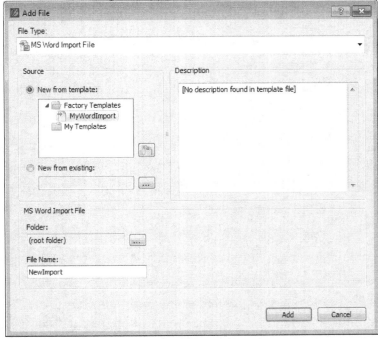

2 For **File Type**, select **MS Word Import File**.

3 Select a **Source** template.

4 Type a **File Name**.

5 Click **Add**.

The MS Word Import Editor appears.

6 Click ⊞.

The Open dialog box appears.

7 Select a Word document and click **Open**.

If needed, you can select more than one Word document.

8 If you plan to continue editing the file in Word, select **Link generated files to source files**.

◇ *This option allows you to link the imported topics to the Word document. When you re-import the document, Flare will replace the original topics with the new topics.*

Linked topics have a chain (⸭) icon after their file name when opened in the XML Editor.

9 Select the **New Topic Styles** tab.

10 Select a style or styles to use to create new topics.

For example, you can create a new topic for each Heading 1 in the Word document.

▥▷ *Flare will automatically create new topics based on manual page breaks in your Word document. You may want to remove manual page breaks before importing.*

11 Select the **Options** tab.

12 If you want to automatically reimport the Word document(s) when you create a target, select **Auto-reimport before 'Generate Output.'**

13 If your Word document uses different headers and/or footers for different sections, select **Create a Page Layout for each section header/footer**.

14 Select the **Stylesheet** tab.

15 Select a stylesheet for the new topic(s).

If you select a stylesheet, Flare will apply the stylesheet to your topics and automatically 'map' styles with matching names. If you do not select a stylesheet, Flare will create a stylesheet based on the formatting in your Word document.

16 Select the **Paragraph Styles** tab.

17 Map (or 'match') your Word heading-level styles to the h1-h6 heading styles.
For example, if you use a first-level heading style named 'HeadText1' in Word, map it to 'h1.' Styles will map to the 'p' (paragraph) style by default.

18 Select the **Character Styles** tab.

19 If needed, map your Word character-level styles to Flare styles. Character-level styles will map to the 'span' tag by default.

20 Click **Import** in the toolbar.
The Accept Imported Documents dialog box appears.

21 Click **Accept**.
The imported topic or topics appear in the Content Explorer in a folder named after the Word import file you used.

Importing DITA documents

You can create a new project based on DITA documents, or you can import DITA documents into an existing Flare project. If you link the imported topics to their source files, you can edit the DITA files and re-import them into your project.

Creating a new project based on a DITA document set

You can create a new project based on a .dita or .ditamap document. If you want to import a DITA document or DITA map into an existing project, see 'Importing a DITA document' on page 74.

When you import a DITA document, Flare saves your settings in a DITA Import File (these files have a .flimpdita extension). You can reuse these settings when you re-import the Word document or import similar documents.

Shortcut	Tool Strip	Ribbon
none	Project > Import Project > DITA Document Set	File > New Project > DITA Document Set

To create a new project based on a DITA document set:

1 Select **File** > **New Project** > **DITA Document Set**.
The Import DITA wizard appears.

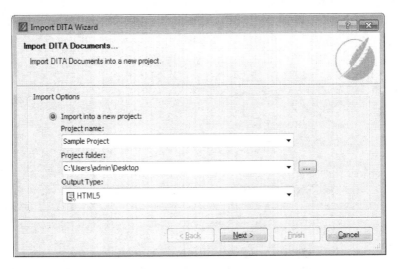

2 Type a **Project Name**.

3 Type or select a **Project Folder**.

4 Select an **Output Type**.
You can add additional output types to your project later.

5 Click **Next**.

6 Click ➕.

7 Select a .dita or .ditamap file and click **Open**.
If needed, you can select more than one DITA document.

8 If you plan to continue editing the original DITA files, select
Link generated files to source files.

◇ *This option allows you to link the imported topics to the source DITA files. When you re-import the document, Flare will replace the original topics with the new topics.*

Linked topics have a chain (⊗) icon after their file name when opened in the XML Editor.

9 Click **Next**.

10 Select **Import all content files to one folder** if you want to import all of the DITA documents into one folder.

11 Select '**Auto-reimport before Generate Output**' if you want to automatically re-import the DITA document(s) when you generate a target.

12 Select **Preserve ID attributes for elements** if you plan to build a DITA target from your project.

13 Click **Next**.

14 Click **Conversion Styles** if you want to change the formatting of your topics.
Flare will create style classes for your DITA tags. You can modify each tag's formatting later in your stylesheet.

15 Select a stylesheet for the new topic(s).
If you select a stylesheet, Flare will apply the stylesheet to your topics.

16 Click **Finish**.

Importing a DITA document

You can import a .dita or .ditamap document into an existing Flare project.

Shortcut	Tool Strip	Ribbon
Alt+P, I, D	Project > Import File > Add DITA Import File	File > New

To import a DITA document or DITA map:

1 Select **File** > **New**.
—OR—
Right-click the **Imports** folder and select **Add DITA Import File**.

The Add File dialog box appears.

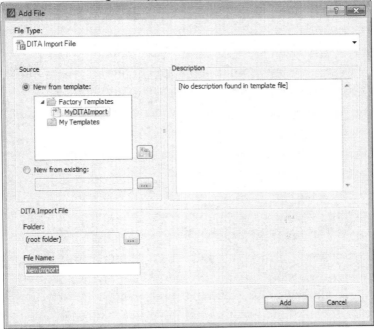

2 For **File Type**, select **DITA Document Set**.

3 Select a **Source** template.

4 Type a **File Name**.

5 Click **Add**.
   The DITA Import Editor appears.

6 Click ![plus button].

7 Select a .dita or .ditamap document and click **Open**.
   If needed, you can select more than one DITA document.

8 If you plan to continue editing the original DITA files, select
   Link generated files to source files.

   ◇ *This option allows you to link the imported topics to the
   source DITA files. When you re-import the document, Flare
   will replace the original topics with the new topics.*

Linked topics have a chain (⚭) icon after their file name when opened in the XML Editor.

9   Select the **Options** tab.

10 Select **Import all content files to one folder** if you want to import all of the DITA documents into one folder.

11 Select **'Auto-reimport before Generate Output'** if you want to automatically re-import the DITA document(s) when you generate a target.

12 Select **Preserve ID attributes for elements** if you plan to build a DITA target from your project.

13 Select the **Stylesheet** tab.

14 Click **Conversion Styles** if you want to change the formatting of your topics.
Flare will create style classes for your DITA tags. You can modify each tag's formatting later in your stylesheet.

15 Select a stylesheet for the new topic(s).
If you select a stylesheet, Flare will apply the stylesheet to your topics.

16 Click **Import** in the toolbar.
The Accept Imported Documents dialog box appears.

17 Click **Accept**.
The imported topic or topics appear in the Content Explorer in a folder named after the DITA import file you used.

Importing HTML and XHTML files NEW!

You can import HTML and XHTML files into a project. If you import an HTML file, Flare will convert it to XHTML.

TIP *If you need to import an Acrobat PDF file, save your PDF file as HTML and import the HTML file.*

To import an HTML or XHTML file:

1 Select **Project** > **Import HTML File Set.**
   The **Import HTML Files** wizard appears.

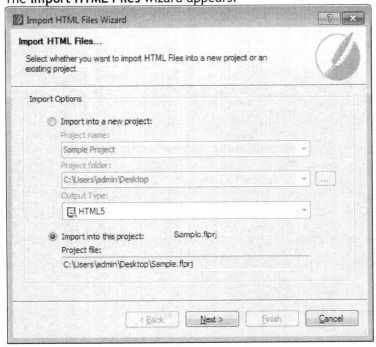

2 Select **Import into this project.**

3 Click **Next.**

4 Click ⊞.

5 Select a .htm, .html, or .xhtml document and click **Open.**
If needed, you can select more than one document.

6 If you plan to continue editing the original file(s), select **Link generated files to source files.**

7 Click **Next.**

8 Select a folder for the imported files.

9 Select **Import linked HTM files** if you want to also import any other files that the selected files link to.
For example, if you import FileA and it links to FileB, this option would also import FileB.

10 Select **Import resources** if you also want to import any files that are used by the selected file(s).
For example, images, stylesheets, or script files used in a topic.

11 If you want to re-import the files when you generate a target, select **Auto-reimport before 'Generate Output.'**

12 Click **Finish.**
The imported topic or topics appear in the Content Explorer in the selected folder.

Importing external resources

You can import files from other locations, such as a network drive, and use them in your project. If you synchronize the files, you can update the source or Flare version when either is modified.

Shortcut	Tool Strip and Ribbon
Alt+V, E	View > External Resources

To import an external resource:

1 Select **View** > **External Resources**.

2 Click ![icon].
The Select Folder dialog box appears.

3 Select the folder that contains the external resource.

4 Click **OK**.
The selected folder appears in the External Resources pane.

5 Select the file(s) you want to import.

6 Click ![icon].
The Select Project Path dialog box appears.

7 Select a folder and click **OK**.
The Copy to Project dialog box appears.

8 If you want to be able to update the file when the source file is modified, select **Keep file(s) synchronized (create mapping)**.

9 Click **OK**.
The file is added to your project. If it is synchronized, it will have a ⊛ icon.

To synchronize external resources:

1   Select **View** > **External Resources.**

2   Click ▓.
    The Synchronize Files dialog box appears.

3   Select **Synchronize Files.**

4   Click **Synchronize.**

5   Click **OK.**

Importing content from Flare projects

You can link projects to reuse files in multiple projects. For example, you can create a template project that contains your stylesheet, page layout, master page, and a 'Contact Us' topic. When you create a new project, you can link the new project to the template project. If you update the files in the source project, you can re-import them into the shared project.

Flare project import files are stored in the Imports folder in the Project Organizer.

Shortcut	Tool Strip	Ribbon
Alt+P, I, P	Project > Import File > Add Flare Project Import File	File > New

To import content from another Flare project:

1   Select **File** > **New**.
    —OR—
    Right-click the **Imports** folder and select **Add Flare Import File**.
    The Add File dialog box appears.

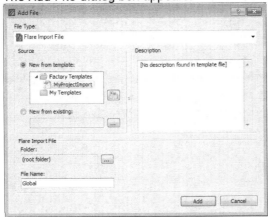

2 For **File Type**, select **Flare Import File**.

3 Select a **Source** template.

4 Type a **File Name**.

5 Click **Add**.

6 Click **OK**.
The Project Import Editor appears.

7 Click **Browse** and select a Flare project (.flprj) file.

8 If you want to re-import the shared files when you generate a target, select **Auto-reimport before 'Generate Output.'**

9 For **Include Files**, select the files or file types to be imported.

10 Select **Auto-include linked files** if you also want to import any files that are used by the selected files (for example, images, stylesheets, or script files used in a topic).

11 For **Exclude Files**, select the file types to not be imported.

12 Click **Import**.

TIP *You can include or exclude multiple files or file types. Here are some examples:*

Entry	Description
overview.htm	only the overview.htm topic
*.css	all .css files (stylesheets) in the project
*.css; overview.htm	all .css files and the overview.htm topic
MyCompany	all files that include 'MyCompany' in their filename
.fl	all Flare-specific files (including TOCs, snippets, page layouts, master pages, and variables)

Lists

You can create bulleted lists to help users scan groups of items, or you can create numbered lists to provide step-by-step instructions. Flare provides the following XHTML list types:

Type	Example
Bulleted list	●
Circle bulleted list	○
Square bulleted list	■
Numbered list	1, 2, 3
Lower-alpha numbered list	a, b, c
Upper-alpha numbered list	A, B, C
Lower-roman numbered list	i, ii, iii
Upper-roman numbered list	I, II, III

You can modify the list styles to change the bullet icon or format the bullets or numbers.

◇ *Flare provides one toolbar button for both bulleted and numbered lists.*

Creating a list

You can select the list type when you create the list.

Shortcut	Tool Strip	Ribbon
Alt+H, U, N	Format > List	▤ ▾ (Home ribbon)

To create a bulleted or numbered list:

1 Open a topic.

2 Position your cursor where you want to create the list.
—OR—
Highlight content that you want to format as a list.

3 Click the ▭ button's down arrow.

4 Select a list type.

5 If you are creating a new list, type the list items.

Sorting a list

You can use the tag bar to sort a list.

To sort a list:

1 Select the list.

2 If you are not viewing the tag bar, click ▭ in the XML Editor's lower toolbar.

3 Right-click the **ol** (numbered list) or **ul** (bulleted list) tag in the tag bar.

4 Select **Sort List** to sort the list.
—OR—
Select **Reverse List** to sort the list in reverse order.

Continuing lists numbers NEW!

If you have two lists, the second list probably restarts with "1." You can continue the numbering in the second list, if needed.

To continue list numbers:

☐ Right-click the second list's ol tag and select **Continue Sequence**.

Tables

You can create tables to organize content and to help users quickly find information. For example, this guide uses tables to present keyboard shortcuts, tool strip buttons, and ribbon commands.

Tables can contain any type of content, including images and lists, and they can be formatted with background shading and borders. You can have as many table rows or columns as you need, and Flare makes it easy to move, add, and delete columns and rows.

Creating a table

Shortcut	Tool Strip	Ribbon
Alt+B, T	▦ (Format toolbar)	Insert > Table

To create a table:

1 Open a topic.

2 Position the cursor where you want to create the table.

3 Select **Insert** > **Table**.
The Insert Table dialog box appears.

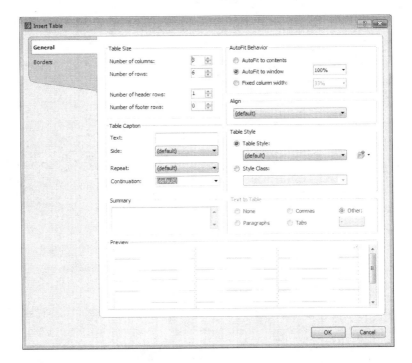

4   Type or select a **Number of Columns**.

5   Type or select a **Number of Rows**.

6   If needed, type or select a number of header and/or footer rows.

7   If needed, type a **Table Caption** and select a caption location.

8   If needed, type a table **Summary**.
    Table captions and summaries are recommended by Section 508 of the U.S Government's Rehabilitation Act and the W3C's Web Content Accessibility Guidelines (WCAG).

9   Select a column width.

    □   **AutoFit to Contents** — each column's width is based on the amount of content it contains.

    □   **AutoFit to Window** — the columns are equally-sized to fit the size of the window.

    □   **Fixed Column Width** — each column is set to a specified width.

10 Click **OK.**

Converting text to a table

You can convert text to a table based on paragraphs, comma, or another character.

Shortcut	Tool Strip	Ribbon
none	Table > Insert > Table	Insert > Table

To convert text to a table:

1 Highlight the text.

2 Select **Insert** > **Table.**

3 In the **Text to Table** group box, select a conversion option.

4 Click **OK.**

Converting a table to text

You can also convert a table to text.

Shortcut	Tool Strip and Ribbon
Alt+B, V	Table > Convert to Text

To convert text to a table:

1 Select the table.

2 Select **Table** > **Convert to Text.**

Sorting table rows

You can sort a table in alphabetical or reverse alphabetical order based on the text in any of the table's columns.

Shortcut	Tool Strip and Ribbon
Alt+B, S, R	Table > Sort Rows

To sort table rows:

1 Click inside the column you want to use for sorting.

2 Select **Table** > **Sort Rows** > **Ascending** or **Descending**.

Rearranging table rows or columns

You can rearrange table rows or columns by dragging and dropping them in the structure bars.

To rearrange table rows or columns:

1 Select a row in the tag bar or a column in the span bar.

2 Drag the row up/down or the column left/right.
A blue arrow will appear.

3 Release the mouse button to move the row or column.

Inserting table rows or columns NEW!

When you insert rows or columns, you can specify whether they're inserted above or below the current row or column. You can also highlight multiple rows or columns to insert multiple rows or columns at the same time.

To insert table rows or columns:

1 Click inside a table. If you want to insert multiple rows or columns, highlight the number of rows or columns you want to insert.

2 Right-click and select **Insert**.

3 Specify columns or rows and above or below.

Creating a table style

In Flare, you can create table styles to format your tables. For example, you can create a table style named 'noBorders' to create tables without borders and another named 'greenHeading' to create tables with a green background for headings.

Table styles are stored in table stylesheets with a .css extension.

Shortcut	Tool Strip	Ribbon
Alt+B, N	(Content Explorer)	File > New

To create a table style:

1 Select **File** > **New**.
  The Add File dialog box appears.

2 For **File Type**, select **Table Style**.

3 Select a **Source** template.

4 Select a **Folder**.

By default, table stylesheets are stored in the Resources/ TableStyles folder.

5 Type a **File Name** for the table stylesheet.

Table stylesheets have a .css extension. If you don't type the extension, Flare will add it for you.

6 Click **Add**.

The Copy to Project dialog box appears.

7 Click **OK**.

The table stylesheet appears in the Content Explorer and opens in the TableStyle Editor.

To modify a table style:

1 Open a table stylesheet.

The TableStyle Editor appears.

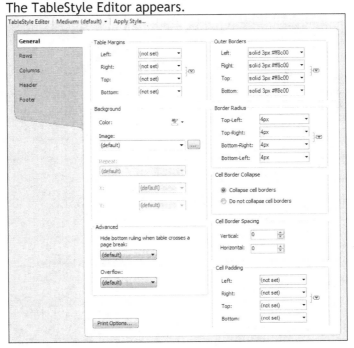

2 On the **General** tab, select the following options:

- ☐ **Outer Borders** — select the style, width, and color of your table borders.

- ☐ **Cell Padding** — select the amount of space between a cell's border and its content.

- ☐ **Table Margins** — select the amount of space between the table and the content around the table.

- ☐ **Cell Border Collapse** — cell borders normally appear inside row borders. If you collapse them, they are merged with the row border.

- ☐ **Cell Border Spacing** — select the amount of space between cells.

3 Select the **Rows** tab.

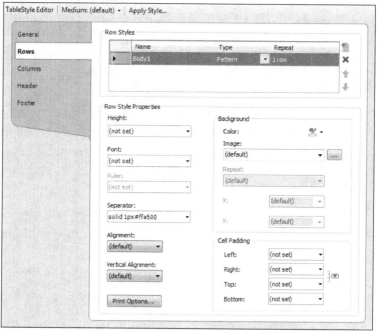

4 On the **Rows** tab, select the following options:

- ☐ **Patterns** — patterns can be used to provide different row formats, such as alternating background colors.

- ☐ **Pattern Properties** — if you use a pattern, select how many times the pattern should repeat, its background color, text color, and a separator border.

5 Select the **Columns** tab.

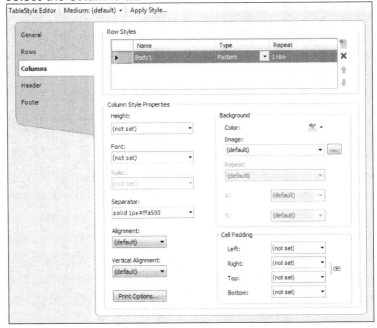

6 On the **Columns** tab, select the following options:

☐ **Patterns** — patterns can be used to provide different column formats, such as alternating background colors.

☐ **Pattern Properties** — if you use a pattern, select how many times the pattern should repeat, its background color, text color, and a separator border.

7 Select the **Header** tab.

8 On the **Header** tab, select the following options:

□ **Patterns** — patterns can be used to provide different header formats, such as a bottom border.

□ **Pattern Properties** — if you use a pattern, select how many times the pattern should repeat, its background color, text color, and a separator border.

9 Select the **Footer** tab.

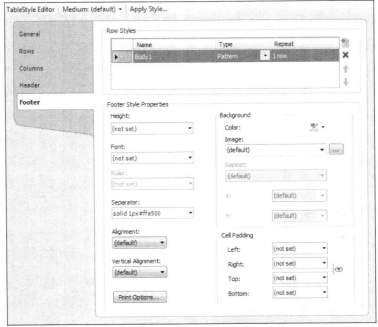

10 On the **Footer** tab, select the following options:

- **Patterns** — patterns can be used to provide different footer formats, such as a top border.

- **Pattern Properties** — if you use a pattern, select how many times the pattern should repeat, its background color, text color, and a separator border.

Applying a table style to a table

After you create a table style, you can apply it to specific tables or all topics in a file, folder, or project.

Shortcut	Tool Strip	Ribbon
Alt+B, P	Table > Table Properties	Table > Apply Table Style

To assign a table style to a table:

1 Click inside the table.

2 Select **Table** > **Table Properties.**
The Table Properties dialog box appears.

3 Select a **Table Style.**

4 Click **OK.**

To assign a table style to multiple tables:

1 Open a table stylesheet.

2 Click **Apply Style.**
The Apply Table Style dialog box appears.

3   Select a topic or folder. If you select a topic, the table style
    will be applied to all of the tables in the selected topic. If you
    select a folder, the table style will be applied to all of the
    tables in the topics stored in the folder.

    *TIP▶ To apply the table style to all of the tables in your
    project, select the Content folder.*

4   Select **Overwrite existing table styles** if you want to apply the
    table style to tables that currently use another table style.

5   Select **Remove local formatting** if you want to also remove
    inline formatting from your tables.

6   Click **OK**.

Removing inline formatting from a table

If a table contains inline formatting, the inline formatting will override
the formatting in your table style. For example, if your table contains
inline formatting that adds red borders, the borders will be red even if
the table stylesheet specifies black borders.

Inline table formatting is often found in topics that are imported from
RoboHelp or Word.

Shortcut	Tool Strip and Ribbon
Alt+B, S, F	Table > Reset Local Cell Formatting

To remove inline formatting from a table:

1 Select **Table** > **Select Table**.

2 Select **Table** > **Reset Local Cell Formatting**.

Deleting a table, row, column, or content

You can press **Backspace** to delete an entire table, table columns, or table rows. If you want to delete content inside a table, you can press **Delete**.

To delete a table:

1 Select the table.

2 Press **Backspace**.

To delete a table row or column:

1 Select the rows/columns.

2 Press **Backspace**.

To delete content in a table:

1 Select the rows/columns.

2 Press **Delete**.

Images, videos, and sounds

You can use any of the following image, video, and sound file types:

Image file types

☐ bmp	☐ hdp (or wdp)	☐ tif (or tiff)
☐ emf (or wmf)	☐ **jpg** (or jpeg)	☐ wdp
☐ eps (or ps)	☐ **png**	☐ xaml
☐ **gif**	☐ svg	☐ xps (or exps)

Video file types

☐ asf (or asx)	☐ mpg (or mpeg)	☐ qt
☐ mov	☐ mimov, miprj, mcmovie, mcmoviesys, and mcmv	☐ **swf**
☐ **mp4**	☐ ogg	☐ **webm**

Sound file types

☐ au	☐ **mp3**	☐ wma
☐ midi (or mid)	☐ wav	

The most popular formats are in bold.

TIP *Capture, MadCap's image editing application, is free and integrates very well with Flare.*

Inserting an image

You can insert images into topics, snippets, master pages, and page layouts. By default, images are stored in the Resources\Images folder.

TIP *You can create a style to display images as small 'thumbnails' that users can enlarge when needed. See 'Creating an image thumbnail style' on page 192.*

Shortcut	Tool Strip	Ribbon
Ctrl+G	▣ (XML Editor)	Insert > Image

To insert an image:

1 Open a file.

2 In the XML Editor, place your cursor where you want to insert the image.

3 Click ▣ in the XML Editor toolbar.
   —OR—
   Select **Insert** > **Image**.

   The Insert Image dialog box appears.

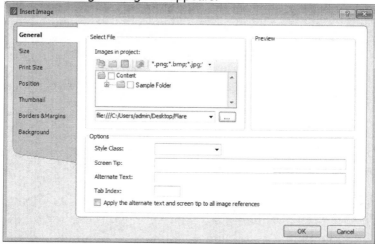

4 Select an image in the Images in Project list.
   —OR—
   Click ⬚ and select an image.

5 Type an **Alternate Text** description of the link.
   Alt text is recommended by accessibility guidelines such as the

US Government's Section 508 and the W3C's Web Content
Accessibility Guidelines (WCAG).

6   Click **OK**.

Inserting a video

You can insert Flash (swf), Windows Media Player (asf and mpg),
QuickTime (mov, mp4, and qt), Mimic, and HTML5 (webm, ogg, and
mp4) videos into topics, snippets, and master pages.

By default, videos are stored in the Resources\Multimedia folder.

Shortcut	Tool Strip and Ribbon
Alt+N, M	Insert > Multimedia

To insert a video:

1   Open a file.

2   In the XML Editor, place your cursor where you want to insert
the movie.

3   Select **Insert** > **Multimedia** and select either:

   □   **Flash** — swf movies

   □   **Windows Media Player** — asf or mpg movies

   □   **QuickTime** — mov or qt movies

   □   **Mimic** — MadCap Mimic mimov, miprj, mcmovie,
   mcmoviesys, and mcmv movies

   □   **HTML5** — mp4, ogg, or webm movies

The Insert Multimedia dialog box appears.

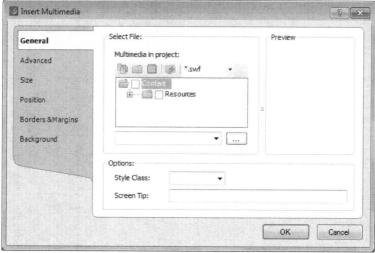

4 Select a movie in the Multimedia in Project list.
   —OR—
   Click [...] and select a movie.

5 Type a screen tip that describes the movie.
   Screen tips are recommended by accessibility guidelines such
   as the US Government's Section 508 and the W3C's Web
   Content Accessibility Guidelines (WCAG).

6 Click **OK**.
   The movie appears in your file as a grey box, but it will play
   normally in the preview and in your targets.

Inserting a sound

You can insert sounds into topics, snippets, and master pages. By
default, sounds are stored in the Resources\Multimedia folder.

Shortcut	Tool Strip and Ribbon
Alt+N, M	Insert > Multimedia

To insert a sound:

1 Open a file.

2 In the XML Editor, place your cursor where you want to insert the sound.

3 Select **Insert >Multimedia > Windows Media Player.**
The Insert Multimedia dialog box appears.

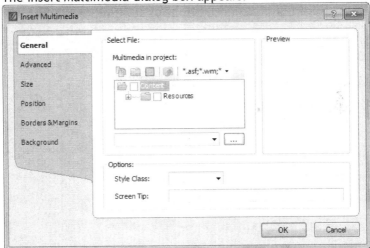

4 Select a sound in the Multimedia in Project list.
—OR—
Click ⌶ and select a sound.

5 Click **OK.**
The sound appears in your file as a grey box, but it will play normally in the preview and in your targets.

'How do I see which files use an image, video, or sound?'

You can right-click any multimedia file and select **View Links** to view a list of topics that include it. In fact, you can right-click any file, including stylesheets, topics, and PDF documents, to see a list of files that include or link to it.

Slideshows ⬡NEW!

You can insert a slideshow to allow users to browse content in a specified order. For example, a slideshow could be used to explain stages in a process or steps in a workflow. Or, you could create a slideshow to provide a graphical list of links. The Flare help system uses a slideshow to provide links to topic-specific PDF guides.

◇ *Slideshows can only be used in online targets. If you are also creating a print target, you should apply a condition tag to the slideshow and exclude it from your print target. See 'Applying a tag to content in a topic' on page 245.*

Inserting a slideshow

You can insert a slideshow into a topic or snippet.

◇ *You cannot insert slideshows inside tables, drop-downs, or togglers.*

Shortcut	Tool Strip and Ribbon
Alt+N, S, S	Insert > Slideshow

To insert a slideshow:

1 Open a file.

2 In the XML Editor, place your cursor where you want to insert the slideshow.

3 Select **Insert > Slideshow**.

Adding a slide to a slideshow

When you create a slideshow, it contains two sample slides. You can modify or delete the sample slides and add additional slides. A slide can contain any content, including text, images, and videos.

To add a slide to a slideshow:

1 Click ✚.
   —OR—
   Right-click the slideshow tag in the tag bar and select **Add Slide**.

2 Click inside the new slide and add your content.

To delete a slide from a slideshow:

1 Click ⬅ or ➡ to select the slide.

2 Click ✖.

Formatting a slideshow

You can set the slideshow's navigation options and each slides' caption, thumbnail icon, and position in the slideshow.

To format a slideshow:

1 Right-click the slideshow and select **Edit Slideshow**.
   The Edit Slideshow dialog box appears.

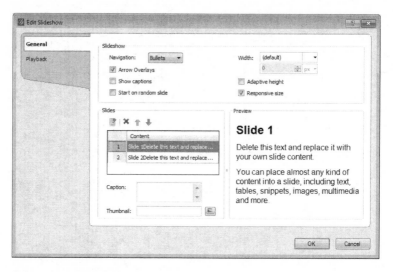

2 Select the **General** tab.

3 Select a **Navigation** option.

4 If you want to provide navigational arrows, select **Arrow Overlays**.
   If you don't provide arrows, users can select slides by clicking the thumbnail icons below the slides.

5 If you want to include slide captions:

   □ Select **Show Captions**.

   □ Select each slide in the Slides group box.

   □ Type a caption.

6 If you want to include slide thumbnails:

   □ Select a slide.

   □ Click .

   □ Select a thumbnail icon and click **OK**.

7   Select the **Playback** tab.

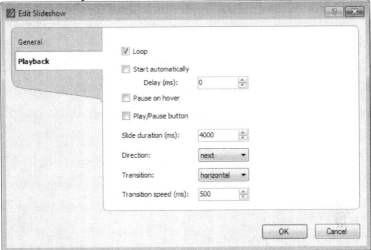

8   Set the playback options.
You can specify whether the slideshow loops, starts automatically, pauses when the user hovers over a slide, and other options.

9   Click **OK**.

Sample questions for this section

1 Which of the following statements is true?
A) You can create HTML or XHTML topics with Flare.
B) You must know HTML or XML to use Flare.
C) XHTML is an XML schema.
D) All of the above.

2 How many topics can you have open in Flare?
A) One
B) Two (one in the XML editor and one in the Internal Text Editor)
C) Up to twenty
D) As many as you want

3 You can import and link the following types of Flare files between projects:
A) Topics
B) Stylesheets
C) Page layouts
D) All of the above

4 How do you import a PDF file?
A) Right-click the **Imports** folder and create a PDF import file.
B) Save the PDF as HTML and import the HTML file.
C) Select **File** > **Import** > **PDF File.**
D) Select **Project** > **Add PDF File.**

5 Table styles files have the following extension:
A) .htm
B) .tss
C) .css
D) .fltbl

6 Which of the following image types can you NOT insert into a topic?
A) jpg
B) svg
C) eps
D) ai

7 How can you view a list of topics that include an image?

A) Select **View** > **Image List**.

B) Right-click the image in the Content Explorer and select **View Links**.

C) Hover your cursor over the image in a topic.

D) Open the Images Analyzer report on the **Project Analysis** tab.

Links

This section covers:

- ☐ Hyperlinks
- ☐ Popup links
- ☐ Cross references
- ☐ Drop-down, expanding, and toggler links
- ☐ Related topic, keyword, and concept links
- ☐ Relationship links

Hyperlinks

You can create hyperlinks that open:

- Topics

- Bookmarks in topics

- Documents such as .doc, .xls, and .ppt files

- PDF files (or even destinations inside a PDF)

- Websites

- Email messages

You can add hyperlinks anywhere in a topic. They are often included at the end of a topic to suggest related topics. A link's text should clearly identify what will happen when it is clicked. For example:

Email technical support (well-worded link label)

Click here if you have a question (poorly-worded link label)

Unvisited links are usually blue and underlined, and visited links are usually purple and underlined. You can change their appearance by modifying the 'a' (for 'anchor') style in your stylesheet.

TIP *If you Ctrl-click a link in the XML Editor, the linked topic, document, or website will open as a new tab in the XML Editor.*

Creating a link to a topic

Shortcut	Tool Strip	Ribbon
Ctrl+K	(XML Editor)	Insert > Hyperlink

To create a link to a topic:

1   Open the topic that will contain the link.

2 Highlight the text that you want to use as the link.
—OR—
Right-click an image and select **Select**.

3 Select **Insert** > **Hyperlink**.
—OR—
Right-click and select **Hyperlink**.
The Insert Hyperlink dialog box appears.

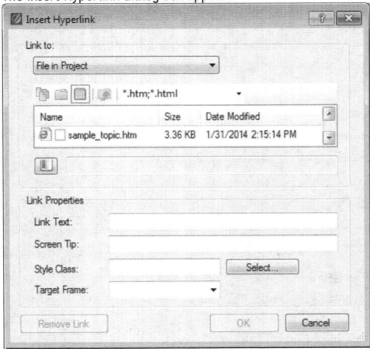

4 In the **Link to** section, select **File in Project**.

5 Select a topic.
▥▷ *You can click the* 🗀 *icon to view the topics organized by folder rather than file name.*

6 If you want to link to a bookmark in the topic:

☐ Click 📖.

☐ Select a bookmark.

☐ Click **OK**.

7   Type a **Screen Tip**.
    Screen tips are recommended by accessibility guidelines such
    as Section 508 of the U.S Government's Rehabilitation Act and
    the W3C's Web Content Accessibility Guidelines (WCAG).

8   If needed, select a **Style Class** for the link.

9   Select a **Target Frame**.
    The target frame specifies where the link will appear. For
    example, you can select 'New Window' to open the link in a
    new window. By default, the link will open in the current
    window.

10 Click **OK**.
    The hyperlink is added to the topic.

Creating a link to a PDF

Shortcut	Tool Strip	Ribbon
Ctrl+K	(XML Editor)	Insert > Hyperlink

To create a link to a PDF document:

1   Locate the document to which you want to link.

2   Copy the document to the Content folder.
    If you want to leave the document in its current location, see
    'Creating a link to a website, external file' on page 118.

3   Open the topic that will contain the link.

4   Highlight the text that you want to use as the link.
    —OR—
    Click an image and select **Select**.

5   Click in the XML Editor toolbar.
    —OR—
    Right-click and select **Hyperlink**.

The Insert Hyperlink dialog box appears.

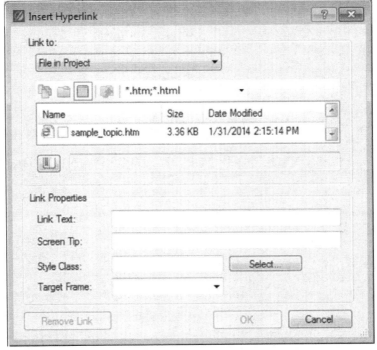

6 In the **Link to** section, select **File in Project**.

7 Select a document. If you do not see your document in the list, you may need to change the filter setting to "All Files."

8 If you want to link to a destination in the PDF:

□ Click 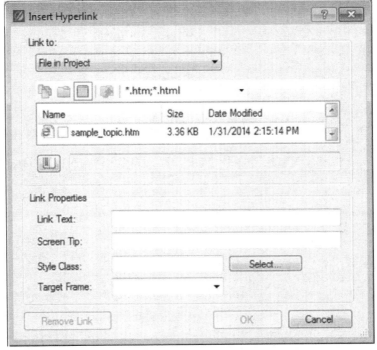.

□ Select a destination.

□ Click **OK**.

9 Type a **Screen Tip**.
Screen tips are recommended by accessibility guidelines such as Section 508 of the U.S Government's Rehabilitation Act and the W3C's Web Content Accessibility Guidelines (WCAG).

10 If needed, select a **Style Class** for the link.

11 Select a **Target Frame**.
The target frame specifies where the link will appear. For

example, you can select 'New Window' to open the link in a new window. By default, the link will open in the current window.

12 Click **OK**.
The hyperlink is added to the topic.

Creating a link to a DOC, PPT, or XLS file

Shortcut	Tool Strip	Ribbon
Ctrl+K	(XML Editor)	Insert > Hyperlink

To create a link to a Word, PowerPoint, or Excel document:

1 Locate the document to which you want to link.

2 Copy the document to the Content folder.
If you want to leave the document in its current location, see 'Creating a link to a website, external file' on page 118.

3 Open the topic that will contain the link.

4 Highlight the text that you want to use as the link.
—OR—
Click an image and select **Select**.

5 Click in the XML Editor toolbar.
—OR—
Right-click and select **Hyperlink**.

The Insert Hyperlink dialog box appears.

6 In the **Link to** section, select **File in Project**.

7 Select a document. If you do not see your document in the list, you may need to change the filter setting to "All Files."

8 Type a **Screen Tip**.
Screen tips are recommended by accessibility guidelines such as Section 508 of the U.S Government's Rehabilitation Act and the W3C's Web Content Accessibility Guidelines (WCAG).

9 If needed, select a **Style Class** for the link.

10 Select a **Target Frame**.
The target frame specifies where the link will appear. For example, you can select 'New Window' to open the link in a new window.

11 Click **OK**.
The hyperlink is added to the topic.

Creating a link to a website, external file, or email address

Shortcut	Tool Strip	Ribbon
Ctrl+K	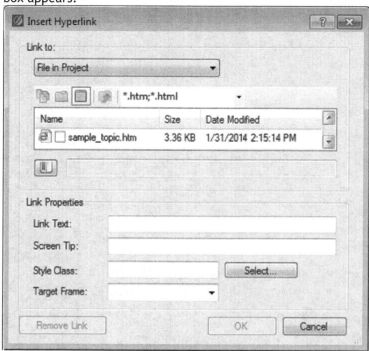 (XML Editor)	Insert > Hyperlink

To create a link to a website or external file:

1 Open the topic that will contain the link.

2 Highlight the text that you want to use as the link.
   —OR—
   Click an image and select **Select**.

3 Click 🖳 in the XML Editor toolbar.
   —OR—
   Right-click and select **Hyperlink**. The Insert Hyperlink dialog box appears.

4 In the **Link to** section, select **Website**.

5   Type the path to the website or document. To create an email link, type 'mailto:' before the email address.

6   Type a **Screen Tip**.
Screen tips are recommended by Section 508 of the U.S Government's Rehabilitation Act and the W3C's Web Content Accessibility Guidelines (WCAG).

7   If needed, select a **Style Class** for the link.

8   Select a **Target Frame**.
Links to websites often appear in a new window.

9   Click **OK**.
The hyperlink is added to the topic.

Creating an image map link

An image map allows you to add links within an image. You can add as many links as needed to an image, and the links can be rectangular, oval, or irregular shapes. For example, you could add links to a picture of the United States so that each state was a link.

To create an image map link:

1   Open the topic that contains the picture to which you want to add links.

2   Right-click the image and select **Image Map**.
The Image Map Editor window appears.

3   If the image appears faded, click ■.

4   Select an image map shape and draw your shape.

5   Double-click your shape.

6   In the **Link to** section, select a link target type, such as a topic or website, and a target.

7   Type a **Screen Tip**.
Screen tips are recommended by accessibility guidelines such as Section 508 of the U.S Government's Rehabilitation Act and the W3C's Web Content Accessibility Guidelines (WCAG).

8 Select a **Target Frame**.

9 Click **OK**.

10 Click **OK** in the Image Map Editor toolbar.
The Image Map Editor closes, and the image map is added to your image.

To apply a condition tag to an image map link: **NEW!**

1 Right-click the image map link and select **Conditions**.

2 Select a condition tag.

3 Click **OK**.

'How do I view a topics' links?'

You can view a list of links by opening a topic (or any type of file) and selecting **View** > **Link Viewer**.

Finding and fixing broken links

You can use the Broken Links analyzer report to find and fix broken links in your project. Broken links are not a common problem, but they can occur when you import content with broken links or if you delete a topic and don't click **Remove Links**.

To find and fix broken links:

1 Select **View** > **Project Analysis** > **Broken Links**.
A list of broken links appears.

2 Double-click a broken link in the list.
The topic opens and the broken link is highlighted.

3 Right-click the highlighted link and select **Edit Hyperlink**.

4 Select a new link location.

5 Click **OK**.

Popup links

You can create two types of popup links: topic popups and text popups.

Topic popups are links that open another topic in a popup window. Since a popup link opens another topic, the popup content can contain formatted text, images, tables, and lists.

Text popups are links that display hidden text in a popup window. They can only contain unformatted text. Since the popup's content is hidden inside the topic that contains the link, you cannot reuse a text popup in multiple topics. Instead, you must retype the content in each topic.

Creating a topic popup link

You can create topic popup links to open topics or other documents in a popup window. They are often used to provide definitions for terms and acronyms.

Like a 'normal' link, a topic popup link opens another topic. The difference is that the topic opens in a popup window that closes when it loses focus. A normal link can open in a new window, but the new window will not automatically close. Flare can automatically size the popup window based on the popup's content, or you can specify the width and height in your stylesheet.

Popup links are also similar to drop-down, expanding, and toggler links. However, drop-down, expanding, and toggler links show and hide content in the current topic rather than in a popup window. Popup links are not as popular as these other link types because they can cause problems with popup blockers and because they can be hard to print. See 'Drop down, expanding, and toggler links' on page 126.

Shortcut	Tool Strip and Ribbon
Alt+N, I, P	Insert > Topic Popup

To create a topic popup link:

1 Open the topic that will contain the link.

2 Highlight the text that you want to use as the link.
   —OR—
   Click an image and select **Select**.

3 Select **Insert** > **Hyperlink** > **Topic Popup**.
   The Insert Topic Popup dialog box appears.

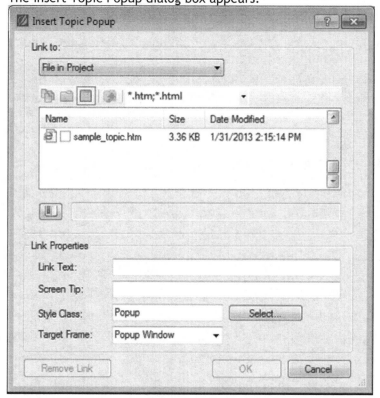

4 In the **Link to** section, select a link target type, such as a topic or website, and select a link target.

5 Type a **Screen Tip**.
   Screen tips are recommended by accessibility guidelines such as Section 508 of the U.S Government's Rehabilitation Act and the W3C's Web Content Accessibility Guidelines (WCAG).

6 Click **OK**.

The popup link is added to the topic.

Creating a text popup link

Text popups can only display unformatted text. The popup's content is stored inside the topic that contains the link, so you cannot reuse a text-only popup in another topic without retyping the popup's content.

Shortcut	Tool Strip and Ribbon
Alt+N, P, U	Insert > Text Popup

To create a text popup link:

1 Open the topic that will contain the link.

2 Highlight the text that you want to use as the link.
—OR—
Click on an image and select **Select**.

3 Select **Insert > Text Popup**.
The Insert Text Popup dialog box appears.

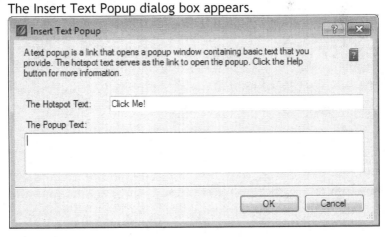

4 Type the popup text.

5 Click **OK**.
The popup link appears.

Cross references

Cross reference links provide two advantages over 'normal' links:

☐ The link's label can use a variable to include the target topic's title

☐ The link's label can include page numbers for print targets

If a cross reference's link label uses a variable to include the target topic's title, the label will be updated automatically if you change the topic's title.

Cross reference labels can be set up using a cross reference style named 'MadCap|xref.' You can set up the style to automatically add words, format, or add page numbers to your cross reference labels.

Creating a cross reference

Shortcut	Tool Strip	Ribbon
Ctrl+Shift+R	🔖 (XML Editor)	Insert > Cross Reference

To create a cross reference:

1 Open a topic.

2 Position your cursor where you want to insert the cross reference.

3 Click 🔖 in the XML Editor toolbar.
   —OR—
   Right-click and select **Cross Reference**.

The Insert Cross Reference dialog box appears.

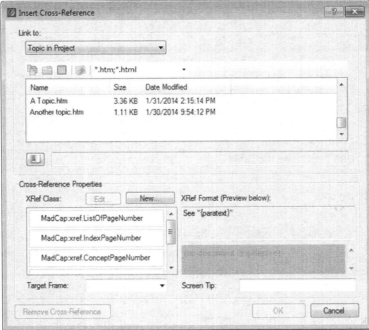

4 For **Link To**, select **Topic in Project**.

5 Select a topic.
▥▶ *You can click the* 📁 *icon to view the topics organized by folder rather than file name.*

6 Click **OK**.

Drop-down, expanding, and toggler links

You can create three types of 'show/hide' links: drop-down, expanding, and toggler. By default, these links can include expanded/collapsed arrow icons. You can change or remove these icons by modifying the link styles.

'What's the difference?'

A **drop-down** link shows and hides a paragraph, image, or list item *below* the drop-down link. Drop-down links are often used to show and hide content between subheadings.

An **expanding** link shows and hides a word or sentence *within* a paragraph or list item. Expanding links are often used to show and hide short definitions.

A **toggler** link shows and hides a named element (such as a paragraph, image, or list item) *anywhere* in a topic. Toggler links are often used to show and hide a screenshot or table from a link at the top of a topic.

Creating a drop-down link

Shortcut	Tool Strip and Ribbon
Alt+N, D	Insert > Drop-Down Text

To create a drop-down link:

1 Open the topic that will contain the drop-down link.

2 Type and highlight the drop-down link and drop-down text.

3 Select **Insert** > **Drop-Down Text.**
The Insert Drop-Down dialog box appears.

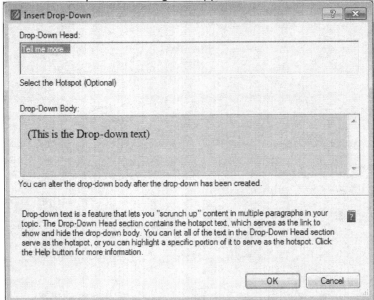

4 Highlight the text you want to use as the drop-down link (or 'head').

5 Click **OK.**
The ⊡ drop-down icon appears to the left of the drop-down link.

Creating an expanding link

Shortcut	Tool Strip and Ribbon
Alt+N, P, T	Insert > Expanding Text

To create an expanding link:

1 Open the topic that will contain the expanding text link.

2 Highlight the expanding link and text.

3   Select **Insert > Expanding Text**.

The Insert Expanding Text dialog box appears.

Insert Expanding Text dialog box

> 🖉 Insert Expanding Text
>
> Expanding text is a feature that lets you "scrunch up" content in a single paragraph in your topic. The hotspot text serves as the link to expand and hide the rest of the text. Click the Help button for more information.
>
> Specify the hotspot by changing the selection:
>
> Click here This is the text that will expand
>
> OK   Cancel

4   Highlight the text that you want to use as the link.

5   Click **OK**.

The 𝕋 expanding text link icon appears after the expanding text link.

Creating a toggler link

Shortcut	Tool Strip and Ribbon
Alt+N, O	Insert > Toggler

To create a toggler link:

1   Open the topic that will contain the toggler link.

2   Right-click the toggler content's block in the tag bar and select **Name**.

3   Type a name for the toggled element.

4   Click **OK**.

5   If needed, assign the same name to other content blocks.

6 In the topic, highlight the text that you want to use as the toggler link.

7 Select **Insert** > **Toggler**.
The Insert Toggler dialog box appears.

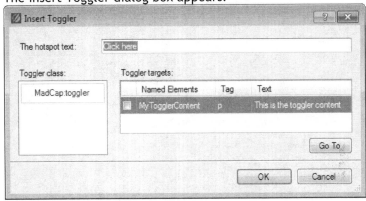

8 Select a toggler target by checking its checkbox.
Remember, you can associate more than one toggler target with a toggler link.

9 Click **OK**.
The ⏻ toggler icon appears to the left of the toggler text.

Related topic, keyword, and concept links

You can add related topic, keyword, and concept (also known as 'see also') links to your topics. When the user clicks one of these links, a popup window appears with a list of topics:

Related topic, keyword, and concept links are automatically removed when you create a print target.

'What's the difference?'

All three of these links open a popup list of topics. The difference between them is how you select the topics that appear in the list.

Related topics links display a list of topics that you have manually selected. They are easier to create than keyword and concept links, but they are much harder to update. If you need to update a related topics link, you must manually add topics to or remove topics from the list.

Keyword links display a list of topics that include the specified index term(s) (or 'keywords'). If you remove a keyword from or add a keyword to a topic, all of the keyword links that use the keyword are automatically updated.

Concept links display a list of topics that include the same concept term. If you remove a concept term from or add a concept term to a topic, all of the concept links that use that concept term are automatically updated.

Creating a related topics link

Shortcut	Tool Strip and Ribbon
Alt+N, R, T	Insert > Related Topics Control

To create a related topic link:

1 Open the topic that will contain the related topics link.

2 Position your cursor where you want to insert the related topics link.

3 Select **Insert > Related Topics Control**.
The Insert Related Topics Control dialog box appears.

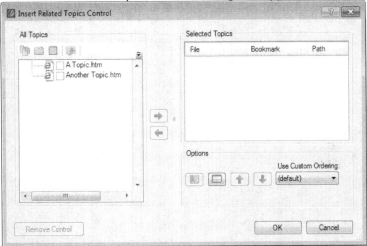

4 Select a topic.

5 Click to add the topic to the related topics link.

6 Add more topics as needed.

7 Click **OK**.
The related topics link appears in your topic.

Creating a keyword link

Before you create keyword links, you will need to add index keywords to your topics. When you create a keyword link, you select a keyword to include all of the topics that contain the keyword. See 'Indexes' on page 157 for information about adding keywords to topics.

Shortcut	Tool Strip and Ribbon
Alt+N, Y	Insert > Keyword Link Control

To create a keyword link:

1 Open the topic that will contain the keyword link.

2 Position your cursor where you want to insert the keyword link.

3 Select **Insert** > **Keyword Link Control**.
The Insert Keyword Link Control dialog box appears.

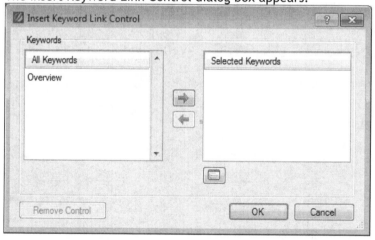

4 Select a keyword.

5 Click to add the keyword to the keyword link.

6 Add more keywords as needed.

7 Click **OK**.
The keyword link appears in your topic.

Keyword links do not work in the preview.

Creating a concept link

Before you create a concept link, you need to add concept terms to your topics. When you create a concept link, you select a concept term to include all of the topics that contain the concept term.

Once advantage of concept links is that you can reuse the terms as search filters. For example, the Flare help system uses numerous concept terms, including 'Best Practices' and 'FAQs.' When you search the help system, you can filter the results to only include topics that contain a selected concept term. For more information about setting up search filters, see 'Adding search filters' on page 169.

Shortcut	Tool Strip and Ribbon
Alt+N, C	Insert > Concept Link

To add a concept term:

1 Open a topic to associate with the concept term.

2 Position the cursor where you want to add the concept term.

3 Select **View** > **Concept Window**.
The Concepts window appears.

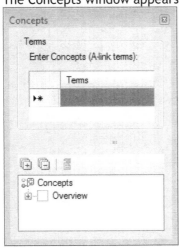

4 Type a concept term and press **Enter**.

5 Type more terms as needed.

6 Click **Save**.

To add a concept link:

1 Open the topic that will contain the concept link.

2 Position your cursor where you want to insert the concept link.

3 Select **Insert > Concept Link**.
The Insert Concept Link Control dialog box appears.

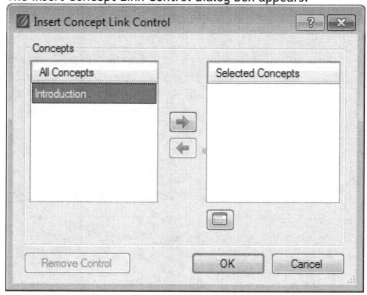

4 Select a concept term.

5 Click ➡ to add the concept term to the concept link.

6 Click **OK**.
The concept link is added to the topic.

◇ *Concept links do not work in the preview.*

Relationship links

You can create relationship tables to organize your topics by type. For example, you can create a relationship table to specify how the following topics are related to each other:

Relationship	Concept	Task	Reference
soccer	defense.htm	goalkeeping.htm	rules.htm
	offense.htm	passing.htm	
		shooting.htm	

This relationship table could be used to add the following links to your topics:

Related Information
- Defense
- Offense

Related Tasks
- Goalkeeping
- Passing
- Shooting

Reference Materials
- Rules

'How are relationship links different from help controls?'

There are four key differences between relationship links and help controls such as related topic, keyword, and concept links:

1 **How they are created and applied**
   Relationship links are created based on relationship tables, and you can associate different relationship tables with different targets.

Help controls are created by manually selecting topics or by automatically selecting topics that contain selected keyword or concept markers.

2 **Link grouping**
Relationship tables are used to specify how topics are related based on topic types such as concept, tasks, and reference. Relationship links can separate links based on their type and display link group headings such as 'Related Information,' 'Related Tasks,' and 'Reference Materials.'

Help controls display the links in one list.

3 **Appearance**
Relationship links appear in the topic.

Help control links appear in a popup window.

4 **Print support**
Relationship links will appear in print targets.

Help control links do not appear in print targets.

Creating a relationship table

You can use one relationship table for your project, or you can create multiple relationship tables and use them for different targets.

Shortcut	Tool Strip	Ribbon
Ctrl+T	📄 (Content Explorer)	File > New

To create a relationship table:

1 Select **File** > **New**.
The Add File dialog box appears.

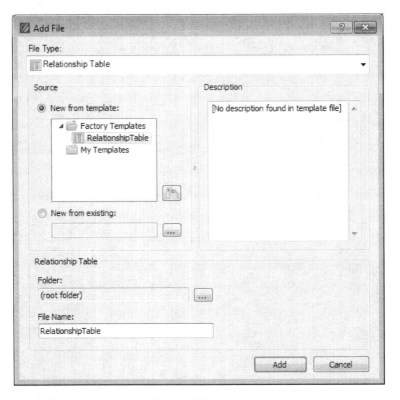

2   For **File Type**, select **Relationship Table**.

3   Select a **Source** template.

4   Type a **File Name**.

5   Click **Add**.

Adding a relationship to a relationship table

Relationships are used to group topics by type. For example, you can create a relationship to group five topics about printing to specify whether each topic is a conceptual, task, or reference topic.

To add a relationship to a relationship table:

1   Open a relationship table.

2   Click to create a new row.

3 Click 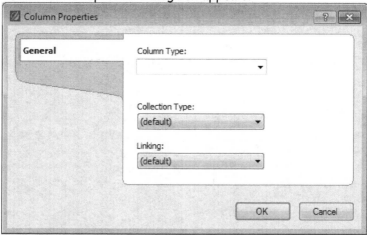.

The Row Properties dialog box appears.

4 Type a name for the row.

5 Click **OK**.

6 Click the **Concept**, **Task**, or **Reference** cell.

7 Click .

8 Select a topic and click **OK**.

Adding a column to a relationship table

By default, relationship tables include concept, task, and reference columns. You can add columns to specify other types of topic relationships.

To add a column to a relationship table:

1 Open a relationship table.

2 Click inside a column.

3 Click .

4 Right-click inside the column and select **Column Properties**.
The Column Properties dialog box appears.

5 Type or select a **Column Type**.

6 Select a **Collection Type**.

Type	Description
Unordered	Creates an unordered list of links.
Family	Creates links to topics in the row and all of the topics in the same cell.
Sequence	Creates links based on their order in the relationship table. This option is only available for DITA topics.
Choice	Allows you to highlight a link in the group. This option is only available for DITA topics.
Use CONREF target	Uses the CONREF attribute determine the links. This option is only available for DITA topics.

7 Select a **Linking** option.

Option	Description
Source Only	The topic will link to other topics, but other topics will not link back to it.
Target Only	The topic will not link to other topics, but other topics will link to it.
None	The topic will not link to other topics, and other topics will not link to it.
Normal	The topic will link to other topics, and other topics will link to it.
Use CONREF target	Uses the CONREF attribute determine the links. This option is only available for DITA topics.

8 Click **OK**.

Renaming a column in a relationship table

You can rename the default 'concept,' 'task,' and 'reference' columns or columns you have added to a relationship table.

To rename a column to a relationship table:

1 Open a relationship table.

2 Click inside a column.

3 Click ⏏.
The Column Properties dialog box appears.

4 Type a new **Column Type**.

5 Click **OK**.

Creating a relationship link

You can add relationship links to your topics to automatically insert links into your topics based on the defined relationships in a relationships table.

Shortcut	Tool Strip and Ribbon
Alt+I, Y, A	Insert > Proxy > Relationships Proxy

To create a relationship link:

1 Open the topic that will contain the relationship link.

2 Position your cursor where you want to insert the link.

3 Select **Insert > Proxy > Relationships Proxy**.
The Relationships Proxy dialog box appears.

Relationships Proxy

You can insert a relationships proxy wherever you want automated topic links to appear in the output. The proxy uses information contained in a relationship table, which indicates how certain topics are related to one another. When you build the output, the proxy is replaced by the generated links.

You can use "Stylesheet class for proxy" if you have created a style class under the tag "MadCap:relationshipsProxy," which can be used to change the look of the relationship links in the output (e.g., provide a special border above them).

Stylesheet class for proxy:

OK   Cancel

4 Click **OK**.

The relationships proxy appears in your topic.

Associating a relationship table with a target

You can create and use different relationship tables for each target to control which links appear in your topics.

To associate a relationship table with a target:

1 Open a target.

2 Select the **Relationship Table** tab.

3 Select the **Relationship Table(s)** to use.

4 Save the target.

Sample questions for this section

1   How can you view a list of topics that link to a topic?
A) Select **Topic** > **Show Links**.
B) Right-click the topic in the Content Explorer and select **View Links**.
C) Right-click the topic and select **Topic Properties**.
D) You can't.

2   How can you find and fix broken links?
A) Click each link in the XML Editor.
B) Select **Project** > **Check Links**.
C) Open the Project Analyzer tab and select the **Broken Links** report.
D) Select **Edit** > **Find and Replace** and search for broken links.

3   What is an image map?
A) A list of all of the images in your project.
B) An image that shows how your topics are linked together.
C) A list of links, like a site map, that users can use to open topics.
D) An image that contains links.

4   How do you change the link label for a cross reference?
A) Change the **Link Label** in the Cross References dialog box.
B) Change the MadCap|xref style properties.
C) Right-click the cross reference and select **Edit Link Label**.
D) You can't—it's always set to the link's topic title.

5   Which type of link can open a web page? (select all that apply)
A) Hyperlink
B) Popup
C) Text popup
D) Cross reference

6   Which type of link can *only* show and hide content below the link?
A) Expanding links
B) Drop-down links
C) Toggler links
D) Drop-down and toggler links

7 Which type of link does not work in Flare's preview window?
   A) Popup links
   B) Cross references
   C) Expanding links
   D) Keyword links

Navigation

This section covers:

- TOCs
- Index
- Search
- Browse sequences
- Glossaries

TOCs

A table of contents ('TOC') is an ordered list of links that your users can use to find and open topics. Most TOCs start with introductory topics and end with troubleshooting and advanced topics.

A TOC contains books and pages. Books are used to organize pages and add levels to your TOC. They can link to topics, or they can simply be used to group pages. Pages always link to topics or other content. A page does not have to be inside a book. For example, a 'What's New' page is often placed at the beginning of a TOC to draw the user's attention.

You don't have to include every topic in your TOC. If you don't include a topic in your TOC, it won't be included when you create a print target.

TOC books and pages usually link to topics, but they can also link to websites, email addresses, other TOCs, browse sequences, and documents such as .doc, .xls, and .pdf files.

TOCs are stored in an XML-based .fltoc file in the Project Organizer.

Moving the TOC to the accordion ⫸

You can move the TOC Editor to the accordion if you want to use your TOC as an alternative to the Content Explorer.

⫸ You can Ctrl-click a book or page in the TOC to open its associated topic in the XML Editor. If you click ▣, you can double-click TOC items to open them in the XML Editor rather than opening the Properties dialog box.

Shortcut	Tool Strip and Ribbon
Alt+W, D	Window > Dock

To dock the TOC Editor:

1 Open your TOC in the TOC Editor.

2 Select **Window** > **Dock**.
   Your TOC will move to the left dock.

Creating a TOC

When you create a project, Flare creates a blank TOC for you. You can use this TOC, or you can create your own.

'Can I create multiple TOCs?'

Yes, you can create multiple TOCs in a project. If you create multiple TOCs, you can use different TOCs for different targets. For example, you can include different topics and organize your topics in a different order for a print and online targets. You can also create multiple TOCs if you have multiple authors. You can link to each author's TOC in a master TOC.

Shortcut	Tool Strip	Ribbon
Ctrl+T	(Content Explorer)	File > New

To create a TOC:

1 Select **File** > **New**.
   —OR—
   Right-click the TOCs folder and select **Add Table of Contents**.
   The Add File dialog box appears.

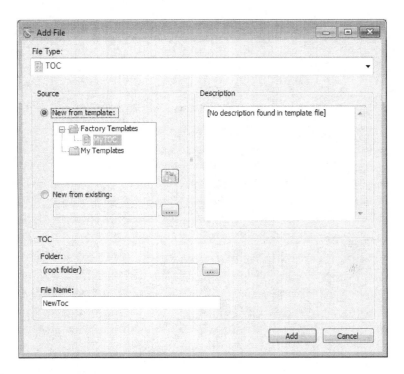

2 For **File Type**, select **TOC**.

3 Select a **Source** template.

4 Type a **File Name**.

5 Click **Add**.
The TOC appears in the TOC folder in the Project Organizer and opens in the TOC Editor.

Creating TOC books and pages

Flare provides multiple ways to create TOC books and pages. You can click the new TOC book or new page icons, type a title, and select a link. Or, you can drag a topic from the Content Explorer to the TOC. You can even drag a folder to the TOC and auto-create a book for the folder and pages for each topic inside the book.

To create a TOC book:

1 Open a TOC.

2 Click 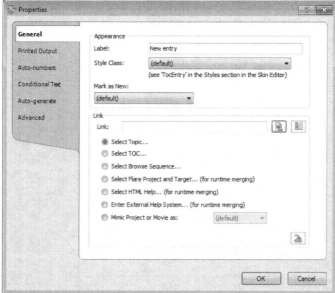 in the TOC Editor toolbar.
A new TOC book named **New TOC Book** appears.

3 Type a name for the book.

4 If necessary, move the book to a new location in the TOC.
You can drag-and-drop the TOC book or use the arrows in the TOC Editor toolbar.

To create a TOC page:

1 Open a TOC.

2 If you want to add a page inside a book, select the book.

3 Click in the TOC Editor toolbar.
A new TOC page named 'New Entry' appears.

4 Double-click the TOC page.
—OR—
Click in the TOC Editor toolbar.

The Properties dialog box appears.

5 Type a **Label** for the page.

6 Click **Select link**.
The Link to Topic dialog box appears.

7 Select a topic.

8 Click **Open**.

9 Click **OK**.

⬖ *A flag ( ) icon appears beside TOC books and pages that are not linked. A broken link ( ) icon appears beside books and pages that have broken links.*

Finding and fixing issues in a TOC

You can find and fix TOC books and pages that are not linked or have broken links.

To find and fix TOC issues:

1 Open a TOC.

2 If your TOC books are intentionally unlinked, click ▮.

3 Click ⚒.
The first issue is highlighted. Unlinked items are marked with a ⚑ icon. Broken links are marked with a ⚒ icon.

4 Right-click the TOC item and select **Properties**.
The Properties dialog box appears.

5 On the **General** tab, select a new link and click **OK**.

Auto-generating TOC books and pages

If you have a long topic with multiple subheadings, you can auto-generate TOC pages to link to the subheadings. For example, the following topic has one main heading and four sub-headings:

South Africa (formatted as Heading 1)
  Cape Town (Heading 2)
  Durban (Heading 2)
  Johannesburg (Heading 2)
  Pretoria (Heading 2)

You can auto-create the following TOC entries for this topic:

South Africa

  Cape Town
  Durban
  Johannesburg
  Pretoria

To auto-generate TOC entries:

1   Double-click a TOC page.
    The Properties dialog box appears.

2   Select the **Auto-generate** tab.

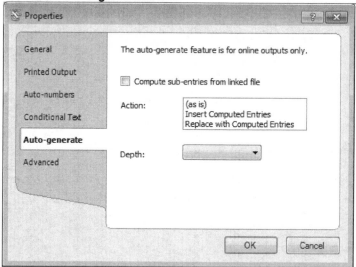

3   Select **Compute sub-entries from linked file.**

4   Select an **Action.**

    □ **Insert Computed Entries** adds the TOC entries below the
       selected TOC entry.

☐ **Replace with Computed Entries** replaces the selected TOC entry with the new entries.

5 Select a heading **Depth**.
The heading depth is the level of subheadings that should be automatically included in the TOC. For example, selecting **2** will include pages for all heading levels 1 and 2.

6 Click **OK**.

Linking TOCs

If you create multiple TOCs, you can create a link from one TOC to another TOC.

To link TOCs:

1 Open a TOC.

2 Select the location in the TOC where you want to add the link to the other TOC.

3 Click ⬚.
A new TOC entry named 'New entry' appears.

4 Select the new entry and click ⬚.
The Properties dialog box appears.

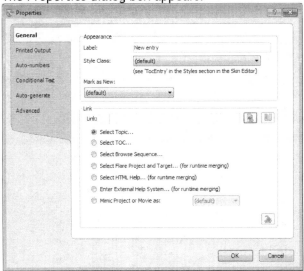

5   Click **Select TOC**.
    The Link to TOC dialog box appears.

6   Select the TOC to which you want to link the page.

7   Click **Open**.

8   Click **OK**.
    The icon in the TOC Editor changes to 🗎, indicating that the page is linked to a TOC.

Deleting a TOC book or page

You can delete books or pages from your TOC. If you delete a book or page, Flare does not delete the topic to which it is linked.

To delete a TOC book or page:

1   Open a TOC.

2   Select a book or page.

3   Press **Delete**.
    The book or page is removed from your TOC.

Applying a TOC to all targets

If you have multiple TOCs, you can select a TOC to be used when you build any target. If you only have one TOC, Flare will automatically associate it with your targets.

To apply a TOC to all targets:

1   Select **Project** > **Project Properties**.
    The Project Properties dialog box appears.

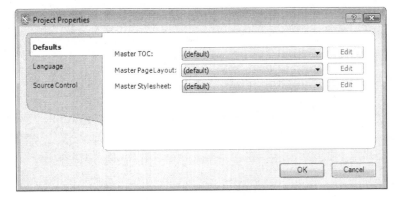

2   On the **General** tab, select a **Master TOC**.

3   Click **OK**.

Applying a TOC to a target

If you have multiple TOCs, you can select a TOC to be used when you build a target. If you only have one TOC, Flare will automatically associate it with your targets.

To apply a TOC to a target:

1   Open a target.

2   On the **General** tab, select a **Master TOC**.

Specifying chapter breaks

If you add chapter breaks to your TOC, you can create separate Word, FrameMaker, or PDF documents for each chapter.

To specify a chapter break:

1   Open your TOC.

2   Right-click a TOC book or page and select **Properties**. The Properties dialog box appears.

3 Select the **Printed Output** tab.

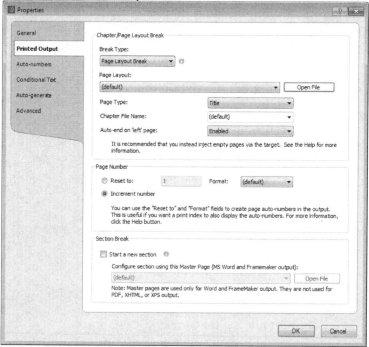

4 For **Break Type**, select **Chapter Break**.

5 Click **OK**.

Finding topics that are not in the TOC

You can use Flare's Analyzer reports to find topics that are not in a TOC. You don't have to include a topic in a TOC, but this report can help you find topics you may have forgotten to include.

To find topics that are not in a TOC:

1 Select **View** > **Project Analysis** > **Topics Not In Selected TOC**.

2 For **Filter**, select a TOC.

TIP▶ *You can double-click a topic in the list to open it in the XML Editor.*

Finding and opening topics from the TOC

When you hover over a TOC book or page, a tooltip will appear that includes the path of TOC item's destination. However, you can also click the Locate file in Content Explorer to quickly find the topic. If you often need to open topics from the TOC, you can set Flare to open topics when you double-click a TOC item.

To find a topic from the TOC: NEW

1 Select a TOC book or page.

2 Click [icon].

To open topics from the TOC when you double-click a book or page:

☐ Click [icon].

Finding topics in the TOC

You can also locate a topic in the TOC. For example, you might move a topic to a new folder in the Content Explorer and decide to also change where it appears in your TOC.

To find a topic in the TOC:

1 Select a topic.

2 Click **Project** > **Locate in TOC**.

Indexes

Like FrameMaker, Flare adds your keywords as markers inside your topics. You can copy a keyword to other topics or delete a keyword when you delete its associated content.

There are four ways to add index entries to topics:

- □ 'Quick term' method
- □ Index Window method
- □ Index Entry Mode method
- □ Auto-index phrase set method

'Why should I create an index?'

Most users will use a search tool instead of an index. An index also takes much more time to create than the search, since you must add index keywords to your topics. However, a good index is more useful that the search because it only lists the most relevant topics. Another key advantage of the index over the search is that the index is included in print targets.

Adding index entries using the 'quick term' method

The quick term method can be used to quickly add a term to the index while you are writing. Because it's so efficient, I often use the quick term method to add index terms.

Shortcut	Tool Strip	Ribbon
F10	Tools > Index > Insert Keyword	Insert > Keyword

To add a term using the quick term method:

1 Open a topic.

2 Click before the word (or highlight the phrase) that you want to insert as an index term.

3 Select **Insert** > **Keyword**.
—OR—
Press **F10**.
The term is added to the index. If you have Show Markers turned on, the term will appear in a green box.

📖▶ *To show markers, click the* 🔖▾ *icon's down arrow in the XML Editor toolbar and select* **Show Markers**. *If you can't see the entire index entry, increase the marker width.*

Adding index entries using the Index window method

The Index window can be used to add single word, multiple word, and second-level index entries. The Index window shows all of the index terms within the current topic.

Shortcut	Tool Strip and Ribbon
F9	View > Index Window

To add an index entry using the Index window:

1 Open a topic.

2 Click before or on the word or phrase that you want to insert as an index term.

3 Select **View** > **Index Window**.
—OR—
Press **F9**.
The Index window appears.

4   Type a term or phrase and press **Enter**.
     The term or phrase is added to the index.

TIP *To add a second-level entry, include a colon between the first- and second-level entries.*

Adding index entries using the Index Entry mode method

Index Entry mode is useful when you need to add multiple index entries. When you switch to Index Entry mode, the words you type become index entries rather than topic content. It's a great tool for indexers, since they can focus on indexing and not worry about accidentally changing the content in a topic.

To add an index entry using Index Entry mode:

1   Open a topic.

2   Click ⓘ in the XML Editor toolbar.

3   Position the cursor where you want to add the index term.

4   Type the term and press **Enter**.
     The Index Entry window appears, and the term is added to the index.

5   Continue typing terms as needed. When you are done, click ⓘ in the XML Editor.

Automatically adding index entries

Instead of adding keywords to topics, you can create an auto-index phrase set to automatically add keywords to your topics when you build a target. This method may cause your targets to build more slowly, but you can share the list of keywords across projects.

◇ *If you plan to link your content to a Word or FrameMaker document, you should use this approach because the keywords are added when you generate a target. If you add keywords using the other methods, they will be removed when you re-import the document.*

Shortcut	Tool Strip	Ribbon
Ctrl+T	📑 (Content Explorer)	File > New

To create an auto-index phrase set:

1 Select **File** > **New**.
The Add File dialog box appears.

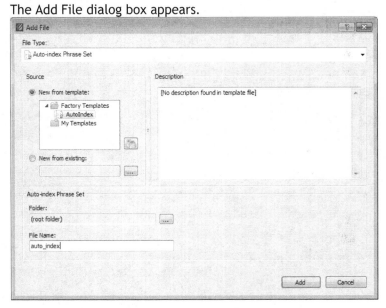

2 For **File Type**, select **Auto-index Phrase Set**.

3 Select a **Source** template.

4 Type a **File Name**.

5 Click **Add**.
The Auto-index Phrase Set is added to the Advanced folder in the Project Organizer and appears in the Auto-index Editor.

To add a term to an auto-index phrase set:

1 Open an auto-index phrase set.

2 Click 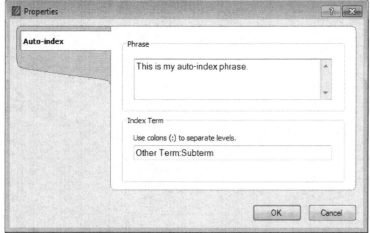.
   The Properties dialog box appears.

3 Type a **Phrase** to find in your topics.
   The phrase can be the term or something more specific to limit
   the number of index markers Flare adds.

4 Type the **Index Term**.

5 Click **OK**.

   ✎ *The phrase and index term are case specific. If you want to
   add a keyword every time the word 'pizza' or 'Pizza' is used in
   your topics, you will need to add two auto-index entries.*

Adding *'See also'* index links

You can create *'See'* or *'See also'* index links to refer one index entry to another index entry.

Shortcut	Tool Strip	Ribbon
Ctrl+T	📑 (Content Explorer)	File > New

To create an index link set:

1 Select **File** > **New**.
The Add File dialog box appears.

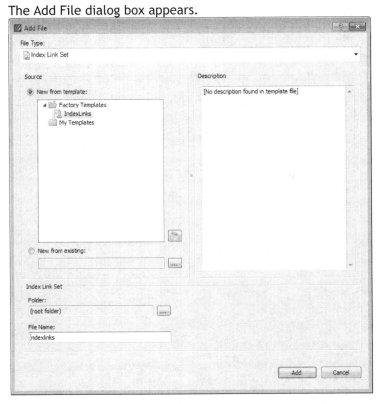

2 For **File Type**, select **Index Link Set**.

3 Select a **Source** template.

4 Type a **File Name**.

5 Click **Add.**

The Index Link Set is added to the Advanced folder in the Project Organizer and appears in the Index Links Editor.

To add a 'see also' entry to an index link set:

1 Open an index link set.

2 Click ⬛.

The Properties dialog box appears.

3 Type an index **Term.**

4 Select a **Link** option.

 ☐   **See** – the 'term' is not linked to any topics. The user should refer to the 'linked term'

 ☐   **See Also** – the 'term' is linked to topics. In addition, the user should also see the 'linked term'

 ☐   **Sort As** – the 'term' should be sorted as indicated by the 'linked term' (ex: '.HTML ' sorted as 'HTML')

5 Type the **Linked Term.**

6 Click **OK.**

Showing or hiding index entries in a topic

Index entry markers can be distracting when you are not indexing a topic. You can hide the index markers using the Show Tags icon in the XML Editor's toolbar.

To show or hide index markers:

1 Click the down arrow beside the ⬖⬖ ▾ icon.

2 Select **Show Markers.**

The index markers disappear.

 TIP *You can change the size of the markers by modifying the Marker Width setting.*

Finding topics that are not in the index

You can use Flare's Analyzer reports to find topics that do not contain index markers.

If you are using an auto-index phrase set, your topics do not contain markers and the report will list all of your topics.

To find topics that are not in the index:

◻   Select **View > Project Analysis > Topics Not In Index**.

You can double-click a topic in the list to open it in the XML Editor.

Viewing the index

Select **View > Index Window** to view the index. All of the index entries and listed at the bottom of the window.

If you are using an auto-index phrase set, your topics do not contain markers and the list will be empty.

Search

It's very easy to add search to an online target: you only need to select one checkbox!

Most users use the search rather than the TOC or index to find information. When a user searches for a word or phrase, a list of all of the topics that contain the search term(s) appears. When the user opens a topic from the search, the search term is highlighted to make it easy to find.

Adding search synonyms

You can add search synonyms to include terms that do not appear in your topics. You can add two types of synonyms: directional and group.

Directional synonyms are used to associate specific terms with general terms. For example, a directional synonym might associate 'country' with 'New Zealand.' If a user searches for 'country,' the search results would include topics that contain 'country' or 'New Zealand.' However, if the user searches for 'New Zealand,' the results would only include topics that contain 'New Zealand.'

Group synonyms are used to associate a group of equivalent words. For example, a group synonym might include 'close,' 'exit,' and 'quit.' If a user searches for any of these terms, the results would include topics that contain any of these words.

Shortcut	Tool Strip	Ribbon
Ctrl+T	📄 (Content Explorer)	File > New

To add search synonyms:

1 Select **File** > **New**.
   The Add File dialog box appears.

2 For **File Type**, select **Synonyms File**.

3 Select a **Template Folder** and **Template**.

4 Type a **File Name**.

5 Click **Add**.
   The synonym file is added to the Advanced folder in the Project
   Organizer and appears in the Synonym Editor.

To add a directional synonym:

1 Open a synonym file.

2 Select the **Directional** tab.

3   Click inside the **Word** cell beside the asterisk (*) and type the
    general term.

4   Click inside the **Synonym** cell and type the specific term.

5   If you want to also search for past tense and plural forms of the
    terms, select the **Stem** option.

To add a group synonym:

1   Open a synonym file.

2   Select the **Groups** tab.

3   Click inside the **Group** cell beside the asterisk (*) and type the
    terms separated by the = sign.
    For example, **close=exit=quit**.

4   If you want to also search for past tense and plural forms of the
    terms, select the **Stem** option.

Excluding a topic in the full-text search

You can hide a topic in the full-text search for WebHelp and DotNet
Help. Many help authors use this feature to hide field-level context-
sensitive help topics in the search.

To exclude a topic in the full-text search:

1   Right-click a topic in the Content Explorer or File List and
    select **Properties**.
    —OR—
    Select a topic and press **F4**.

2   Select the **Topic Properties** tab.

3   Deselect the **Include topic when full-text search database is
    generated** option.

4   Click **OK**.

Adding meta descriptions

A meta description is a brief summary of a topic. You can add meta descriptions to improve your content's results in search engines such as Google. Meta descriptions also appear in the HTML5 search results list. If you don't add meta descriptions, the content at the beginning of the topic will be used as the description.

◇ *Meta descriptions should be a maximum of 155 characters.*

To add a meta description to a topic:

1 Right-click a topic in the Content Explorer or File List and select **Properties**.
–OR–
Select a topic and press **F4**.

2 Select the **Topic Properties** tab.

3 Type a **Description**.

4 Click **OK**.

Using search filters

You can use search filters to allow your users to search within a subset of your content. For example, you could add a search filter to allow user to only search installation or troubleshooting topics.

To add search filters, you will need to:

☐ Add concept terms to your topics (see 'Creating a concept link' on page 133)

☐ Create a search filter set

☐ Use search filters in a target

To create a search filter set:

1 Select **File** > **New**.
The Add File dialog box appears.

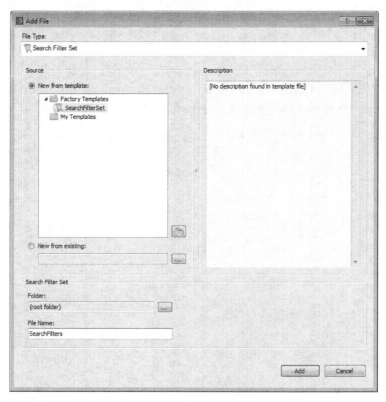

2 For **File Type**, select **Search Filter Set**.

3 Select a **Template Folder** and **Template**.

4 Type a **File Name**.

5 Click **Add**.
The search filter set is added to the Advanced folder in the Project Organizer and appears in the SearchFilterSet Editor.

6 Double-click the 'NewFilter' filter and type a new name. Examples: 'FAQs', 'Version 2,' 'Advanced Features'

7 Double-click the empty **Concepts** cell.
The Select Concepts for Search Filter dialog box appears.

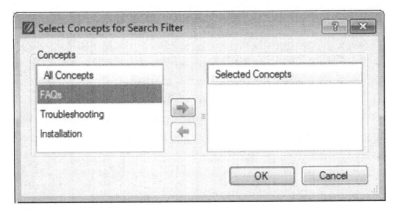

8 Select a **Concept** term.

9 Click ⟹.

10 Click **OK**.

11 Click 📄 to add another filter.

12 Follow steps 7-11 to set up each filter.

To use a search filter in a target:

1 Open an online target.

2 Select the **Advanced** tab.

3 For **Search Filters**, select your filter.

Glossaries

Flare provides two glossary features: a combined glossary tab/page that lists all of the terms and definitions, and glossary links that open definitions from your topics.

Glossary terms are stored in a glossary file with a .flglo extension. Glossary files are stored in the Glossaries subfolder in the Project folder.

Creating a glossary

You can use multiple glossaries in a project. For example, you can maintain a glossary of common terms that is shared across multiple projects and another glossary of project-specific terms.

Shortcut	Tool Strip	Ribbon
Ctrl+T	📄 (Content Explorer)	File > New

To create a glossary:

1 Select **File** > **Add**.
   The Add File dialog box appears.

2 For **File Type**, select **Glossary**.

3 Select a **Source** template.

4 Type a **File Name**.
   Glossaries have a .flglo extension. If you don't type the extension, Flare will add it for you.

5 Click **Add**.
   The glossary appears in the Glossaries folder in the Project Organizer and opens in the Glossary Editor.

Adding glossary terms

You can add terms and definitions directly to a glossary or as you write topics. If you need to include formatting or an image in a definition, you can link to a topic for the definition.

1 Open a glossary.
Glossaries are stored in the Glossaries folder in the Project Organizer.

2 Click 📄 in the Glossary Editor toolbar.
The Properties dialog box appears.

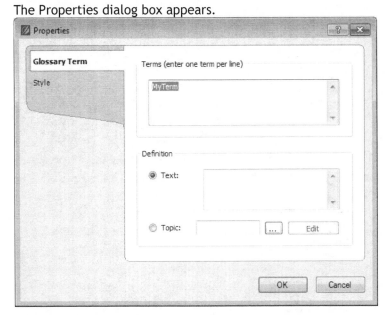

3 Type a glossary **Term**.

4 Type a **Definition** or select a topic that contains the definition.

5 Select the **Style** tab.

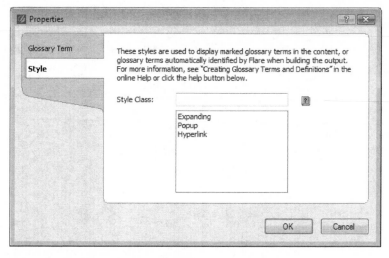

6   Select a style for the glossary link:

   ☐ **Expanding** — opens the definition with an expanding link

   ☐ **Popup** — opens the definition in a popup window

   ☐ **Hyperlink** — closes the current topic and opens the
      glossary page

   ◇ *If you don't select a style, Flare will use the 'Popup'*
   style.

7   Click **OK**.

Adding a glossary to a target

To use a glossary in a target, you need to enable it in a skin and
associate the skin with a target. You can use different glossaries in
different targets, or you can use multiple glossaries in the same target.

To enable a glossary in a skin:

1   Open a skin.

2   On the **General** tab, select the **Glossary** option.

To associate a glossary with a target:

1 Open a target.

2 Select the **Glossary** tab.

3 If you want to include glossary links in your topics, select a **Glossary Term Conversion** method.

4 Select a **Glossary File**.

5 Click **Save**.

'Where's the HTML Help glossary tab?'

HTML Help does not include a glossary tab, and MadCap cannot add one without requiring a .dll file. So, your glossary appears at the bottom of the TOC and opens on the right in the topic pane.

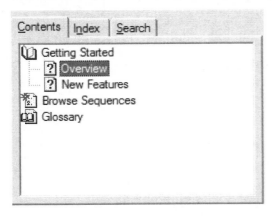

Browse sequences

Like a TOC, a browse sequence is an ordered list of links that can be used to find and open topics. It even uses books and pages like a TOC.

You can create a browse sequence if you want to provide an alternate TOC for your users. For example, you could organize your TOC for technical support users and your browse sequence for managers. Or, you could organize your TOC by complexity (introductory topics first and troubleshooting topics last) and your browse sequence alphabetically.

Browse sequences are stored in a browse sequence file with a .flbrs extension. Browse sequence files are stored in the Advanced subfolder in the Project folder.

Creating a browse sequence

Shortcut	Tool Strip	Ribbon
Ctrl+T	▤ (Content Explorer)	File > New

To create a browse sequence:

1 Select **File** > **New**.
   The Add File dialog box appears.

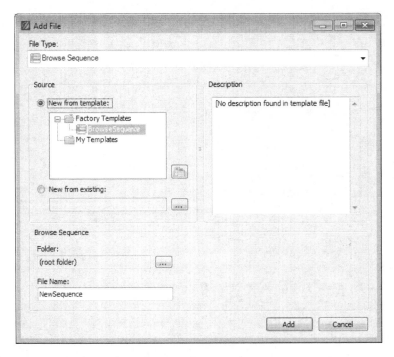

2   For **File Type**, select **Browse Sequence**.

3   Select a **Source** template.

4   Type a **File Name** for the browse sequence.
    Browse sequences have a .flbrs extension. If you don't type the
    extension, Flare will add it for you.

5   Click **Add** and click **OK**.
    The browse sequence appears in the Advanced folder in the
    Project Organizer and opens in the Browse Sequence Editor.

To add books to a browse sequence:

1   Open the browse sequence.

2   Open the Content Explorer.

3   Drag a folder from the Content Explorer to the browse sequence.

4   If you need to rename the browse sequence book:

- Click the selected new book entry.
  —OR—
  Press **F2**.
  The text for the entry is highlighted.

- Type the new name.

To manually add books to a browse sequence:

1 Open the browse sequence.

2 Click or in the Browse Sequence Editor toolbar. A book named 'New TOC Book' is added to the browse sequence.

3 Click the selected new book entry.
  —OR—
  Press **F2**.
  The text for the entry is now highlighted.

4 Type a name for the book.

To add pages to a browse sequence using drag-and-drop:

1 Open the browse sequence.

2 Open the Content Explorer.

3 Drag a topic from the Content Explorer to the browse sequence.

4 If necessary, use the arrows in the browse sequence toolbar to move the page up, down, left or right.

← → ↑ ↓

To add pages to a browse sequence using the Browse Sequence Editor:

1 Open the browse sequence.

2 Select the location in the browse sequence where you want to add the new entry.

3 Click 📄 in the Browse Sequence Editor.
An entry named 'New entry' is added to the browse sequence.

4 Click the selected new entry.
—OR—
Press **F2**.
The text for the entry is now highlighted.

5 Type a name for the entry and press **Enter**.

6 If necessary, use the arrow buttons in the browse sequence toolbar to move the page left, right, up, or down.

7 Double-click the new entry.
The Properties dialog box appears.

8   If needed, select the **Mark as New** option.
The page will be marked with the 'New' icon: ▢. You can change this icon in your skin.

9   Select **Select Topic**.

10 Click **Select Link**.
The Link to Topic dialog box appears.

11 Select a topic and click **Open**.

12 Click **OK**.

Creating a browse sequence based on your TOC 📑▶

Since Flare uses XML for the TOC and browse sequence files, you can make a copy of your TOC and convert it to a browse sequence.

To create a browse sequence based on your TOC:

1   In Windows Explorer, create a copy of your TOC file.
By default, TOC files are located in the Project\TOCs folder.

2   Paste the copy of your TOC file into the Project\Advanced folder.

3   Change the TOC file's extension from .fltoc to .flbrs.
The Rename dialog box appears.

4   Click **Yes**.
Your new browse sequence appears in the Advanced folder in the Project Organizer.

Using a browse sequence

To use a browse sequence, you need to enable it in a skin and associate it with a target. You can use different browse sequences in different targets, or you can use multiple browse sequences in the same target.

To enable a browse sequence in a skin:

1 Open a skin.

2 On the **General** tab, select the **Browse Sequence** option.

3 If you want to include 'next' and 'previous' browse sequence buttons in the WebHelp or Topic toolbar:

   ❑ Select the **WebHelp Toolbar** or **Topic Toolbar** tab.

   ❑ Add the **NextTopic, PreviousTopic**, and/or **CurrentTopicIndex** items to your toolbar.

The three items appear as follows (previous, current, and next):

To associate a browse sequence with a target:

1 Open a target.

2 On the **General** tab, make sure the browse sequence is enabled in the selected skin.

3 Select a **Browse Sequence.**

'Where are my HTML Help browse sequences?'

HTML Help does not include a separate browse sequence feature. Some tools, such as RoboHelp, use a .dll file to add browse sequences to HTML Help. MadCap does not want to require a .dll file for HTML Help, so Flare adds your browse sequence to the bottom of your TOC.

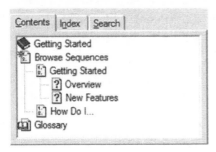

Sample questions for this section

1 Where are TOC files stored?
A) In the Content Explorer's TOCs folder
B) In the Content Explorer's Resources\TOCs folder
C) In the Project Organizer's TOCs folder
D) In the TOC Explorer

2 Which statement about a TOC is NOT true?
A) Pages must be inside books.
B) Pages can link to topics, Word documents, and web sites.
C) Books can link to topics.
D) Books can contain books.

3 Which character is used to separate first- and second-level index entries?
A) |
B) /
C) :
D) ;

4 How can you view a list of your index terms?
A) Double-click your index in the Project Organizer.
B) Double-click your index in the Content Explorer.
C) Open the Analyzer index report.
D) Select **View** > **Index Window.**

5 How do you exclude a topic in the search?
A) Add the topic to your search file in the Project Organizer.
B) Open the Topic Properties dialog box and deselect the **Include topic when full-text search database is generated** option.
C) Do not include the topic in your TOC.
D) You cannot exclude a topic from the search.

6 Where does the glossary appear in HTML Help?
A) As a Glossary accordion item
B) As a Glossary tab
C) At the bottom of the table of contents
D) The glossary does not appear in HTML Help.

7 What is a browse sequence?

A) The path the user used to open the topic.

B) An ordered list of links that can be used to find and open topics, like a TOC.

C) A list of related topics at the bottom of topics.

D) A path at the top of your topics that shows how to find this topic in the TOC.

Format and design

This section covers:

- ☐ Stylesheets
- ☐ Master pages
- ☐ Page layouts
- ☐ Skins
- ☐ Responsive output **NEW!**

Stylesheets

Like Word templates and FrameMaker catalogs, stylesheets are used to format content. You can define the formatting for each style in a stylesheet, and you can add your own styles (called 'classes') to a stylesheet. You can even specify print- and online-specific styles within a stylesheet to use different formatting for print and online targets.

Stylesheets are stored in the Content Explorer. By default, stylesheets created in Flare are stored in the Resources\Stylesheets folder. If needed, you can move a stylesheet to a different folder.

External and inline styles

Styles that are defined in your cascading stylesheet are called 'external' styles because the formatting information is stored in another file rather than in your topics.

You can also format your content directly by highlighting content and changing its appearance. For example, you can highlight a word and make it bold and red. This type of formatting is called 'inline' formatting because the formatting information is stored directly in the topic.

You should avoid using inline formatting. It is much harder to change inline formatting than it is to change a style. If you change a style, all of the topics that use the style are automatically updated when you save the stylesheet. If you need to change inline formatting, you have to change it by hand. Another problem is that inline formatting overrides your styles. It is hard to maintain consistent formatting if you have scattered inline formatting throughout your topics.

If you have inline formatting, you can remove it or convert it to a style. See 'Removing inline formatting from a table' on page 97,' 'Removing inline formatting' on page 197, and 'Converting inline formatting to a style class' on page 191 for more information.

Creating a stylesheet

Although most Flare projects use the same stylesheet for all topics, you can create multiple stylesheets and apply them to different topics. For example, you could create a 'New Feature' stylesheet so that new topics in your project stand out to your users.

Shortcut	Tool Strip	Ribbon
Ctrl+T	(Content Explorer)	File > New

To create a stylesheet:

1 Select **File** > **New**.
The Add File dialog box appears.

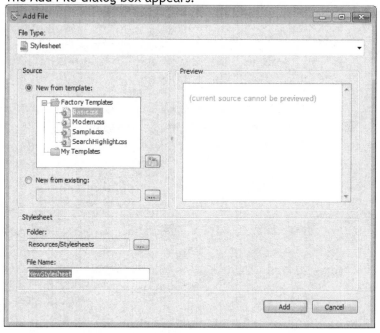

2 For **File Type**, select **Stylesheet**.

3 Select a **Source** template.

4 Type a **File Name** for the stylesheet.
Stylesheets have a .css extension. If you don't type the extension, Flare will add it for you.

5 Click **Add.**

The Copy to Project dialog box appears.

6 Click **OK.**

The stylesheet appears in the Content Explorer and opens in the Stylesheet Editor.

Creating a new style class

You can create your own style classes to format notes, warnings, or other types of content. Most style classes are based on the p (paragraph) tag, but you can also create classes for headings, lists, and tables.

To create a style class:

1 Open the stylesheet.

The Stylesheet Editor appears.

2 Select a style.

For example, to create a paragraph style class, select **p.**

3 Click **Add Class.**

4 Type a name for the style class.

5 Click **OK.**

Creating an auto-numbering style

You can create an auto-numbering style to automatically number content, including headings, captions, and figures. Auto-numbering styles are often used in print documents.

To create an auto-numbering style:

1 Open the stylesheet.

The Stylesheet Editor appears.

2 Select a style.

For example, to create a paragraph style class, select **p.**

3 Click **Add Class.**

4 Type a name for the style class.

5 Click **OK**.

6 Select the new style class.

7 If you are using the Simplified View:

□ Double-click the style class.

□ Select the **Auto-number** tab.

If you are using the Advanced View:

□ In the Show group, select **Property Groups**.

□ Open the **AutoNumber** property group.

□ Select the **(not set)** value for the **mc-auto-number** property.

8 Type or select an auto-numbering format.

Example	Auto-number Format
1.0 (sample text) 2.0 (sample text)	A:{n+}.{ =0}

I.
    1.1
    1.2
	A:{n}.{n+}

I. II.	O:{R+}.

I.
    A.
    B.
	O:{ }{A+}.

Chapter 1	CH:Chapter {chapnum}
Figure 1-1	CF: Figure {chapnum}-{n+}

9 Click **OK**.

10 Click **Save**.

Creating a redacted content style

You can create a redacted content style to 'black out' sensitive, confidential, or private content in a PDF or XPS target. When you apply a redacted style to text, images, or other content, it is permanently replaced with a black rectangle. Users cannot view the original content.

TIP *You can also use a redacted content style to highlight (rather than black out) content in a PDF or XPS target.*

To create a redacted content style:

1 Open the stylesheet.
The Stylesheet Editor appears.

2 Select a style.
For example, to create a paragraph style class, select **p**.

3 Click **Add Class**.

4 Type a name for the style class.

5 Click **OK**.

6 Select the new style class.

7 If you are using the Simplified View:

☐ Double-click the style class.

☐ Select the **Advanced** tab.

If you are using the Advanced View:

☐ In the Show group, select **Property Groups**.

☐ Open the **Redaction** property group.

☐ Select the **(not set)** value for the **mc-redacted** property.

8 Select **Redacted**.

9 Click **Save**.

To select how redacted content appears in a PDF or XPS target:

1   Open the target.
    The Target Editor appears.

2   Select the **Print Output** tab.

3   Select a **Redacted Text** option: blackout, highlighted, or
    normal.

Creating a "Note" style NEW!

You can create a style that automatically adds text, such as the word
"Note:" before your content.

To create a "Note" style:

1   Open the stylesheet in the Advanced View.
    The Stylesheet Editor appears.

2   Select the **p** style.

3   Click **Add Pseudo Class**.
    The New Pseudo Class dialog box appears.

4   Select **Before**.

5   Click **OK**.

6   Select the **before** pseudo style class.

7   Select the **(not set)** value for the **content** property.

8   Type your content.
    For example, type Note:

Selecting a color

You can select an RGB or CMYK color for text colors or background
colors to customize styles, page layouts, and skins. Flare maintains a
list of recently-used colors, and you can even save colors that you use
often.

To select a color for a style:

1 Open the stylesheet.
The Stylesheet Editor appears.

2 If you are using the Simplified View:

☐ Double-click a style.

☐ Select the **color** or **background** property.

If you are using the Advanced View:

☐ Select the (not set) value for the **color** or **background-color** property.

3 Select **More Colors**.
The Color Picker dialog box appears.

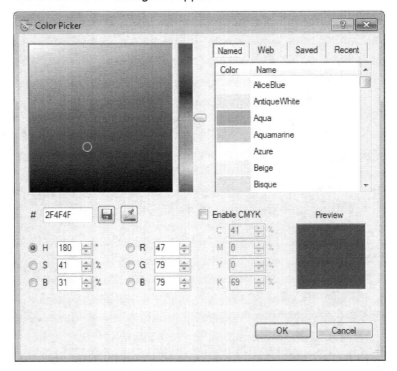

4 Select one of the following:

☐ to select a color from your screen.

☐ **Named** to select a named color as defined by the W3C.

- □ **Web** to select a web-safe color.
- □ **Recent** to select a recently-used color.
- □ **Saved** to select a saved color.

5 If you want to use a CMYK color, select **Enable CMYK**.

TIP *If you select a CMYK color, you can convert it to RGB for print targets. See 'Setting up a print target' on page 264.*

6 If you want to save your color, click 💾.

7 Click **OK**.

Creating an image thumbnail style

You can create a thumbnail style to display smaller 'thumbnail' versions of your images in your targets, and you can specify whether the image displays as full size when the user clicks or moves their mouse over an image.

✎ *You can click 🖼 ▾ and select **Show All Images As Thumbnails** to view all images as thumbnails in the XML Editor.*

To create an image thumbnail style:

1 Open the stylesheet.
The Stylesheet Editor appears.

2 Select the **img** style or an img style class.

3 Click **Add Class**.

4 Type a name for the style class.

5 Click **OK**.

6 Select the new style class.

7 If you are using the Simplified View:

- □ Double-click the style class.
- □ Select the **Thumbnail** tab.

- Select a **Thumbnail** value:

  - **hover** - the image appears in a popup window when the user hovers the mouse over the thumbnail

  - **link** - the image appears in a new window when the user clicks the thumbnail

  - **popup** - the image appears in a popup window when the user clicks the thumbnail

- Select a **Max Width** or **Max Height**.
  The default setting is a height of 48px. Flare will proportionately scale the image, so you don't need to set both properties.

- Click **OK**.

If you are using the Advanced View:

- In the Show group, select **Property Groups**.

- Open the **Thumbnail** property group.

- Select a value for the **mc-thumbnail** property.

- Select a value for the **mc-thumbnail-max-height** or **mc-thumbnail-max-width** property.
  The default setting is a height of 48px.

- Click **Save**.

Converting inline formatting to a style class

You can create a style class based on inline formatting. This approach is useful for removing inline formatting or if you prefer to see your formatting as you design it. You can create a style class in the Stylesheet Editor, but sometimes it's easier to create a style by seeing how it will look in your topics.

To create a style based on inline formatting:

1 Open a topic in which you want to use the new style.

2 Use the formatting options on the **Home** ribbon to format the text.

3 Click inside the formatted content.

   ◇ *If you want to create a character style, highlight the formatted content. If you want to make a paragraph style, do not highlight the content.*

4 Select **Home** > **Style Window.**
   —OR—
   Press **F12.**
   The Style window appears.

5 Click **Create Style.**
   The Create Style dialog box appears.

6 In the **Name** field, type a name for the new style without using spaces.

7 If you do not want to include a style property in the new style, deselect its **Include** option.

8 If you want the new style to be applied to the selected content, select **Create style and update the source element.**

   If you do not want the new style to be applied to the selected content, select **Create style without updating the source element.**

9 Click **OK**.
The new style is added to the stylesheet.

Removing inline formatting

You can remove inline formatting from a topic to 'clean up' the formatting. This feature is especially useful if you import a Word or FrameMaker document that uses a lot of inline formatting.

Removing inline formatting does not change how your content is tagged: headings, lists, and tables will not become paragraphs.

To remove inline formatting:

1 Open a topic that contains inline formatting.

2 Highlight the content that contains inline formatting. You can press **Ctrl+A** to highlight the entire topic.

3 Click ℬ.

Modifying a style

You can use Flare's Stylesheet Editor to modify a style's properties.

To modify a style:

1 Open a stylesheet.
The Stylesheet Editor appears.

2 Select the style you want to edit.
If you are using the Advanced view, the selected style's properties appear on the right. If you are using the Simplified view, double-click the style.

3 Select a property.

4 Select a value to change.

5 Type or select a new value.

6 Modify other properties as needed.

Adding curved borders NEW!

You can add curved borders to tables or to any type of content, such as a "note" paragraph style. Microsoft Word and browsers that don't support curved borders will display square corners, but they are supported in most browsers and in PDFs.

To add curved borders:

1 Open a stylesheet.
The Stylesheet Editor appears.

2 Select the style you want to edit.

3 Open the **Custom** property group.

4 Set the **border-radius** property.

Creating a font set

You can create a font set to specify a list of fonts for a style to use rather than one font family. If you specify a font that is not installed on the user's computer, their browser will use a default font (usually Times). With a font set, you can provide a list of fonts to try before the default font is used.

If you are developing HTML Help or DotNet Help, you should create a font set if you want to use fonts that are not common in Windows. If you are developing WebHelp or HTML5, you should create a font set if you want to use fonts that are not common in Windows or if your users have Mac or Linux computers. Fonts that are commonly installed in Windows might not be available in other operating systems.

To create a font set:

1 Open any topic.

2 Select the **Home** ribbon and click the ⬒ arrow button in the **Font** section.
—OR—
Press **Ctrl+Shift+B**.

The Font Properties dialog box appears.

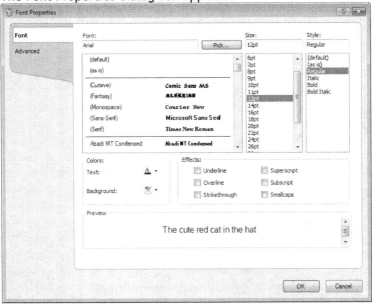

3 Click **Pick**.

The Font Picker dialog box appears.

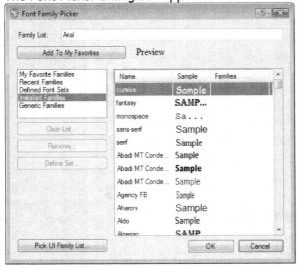

4 Select **Defined Font Sets**.

5 Click **Define Set**.

6 Type a **Name** for the font set.

7 In order, select the fonts you want to include and add them to the list.

8 Click **OK** three times.

You can now use your font set when you select a font for your styles.

Using the print medium

Flare's built-in 'print' medium is often used when creating print targets. For example, you can set up the print medium to use a different font than online targets.

I often use the print medium to set automatic page breaks for heading 1s and to format my TOC and index styles.

To set automatic page breaks before headings:

1 Open your stylesheet.
Stylesheets are stored in the Resources folder in the Content Explorer.

2 Click **Advanced View.**

3 Select the **Print** medium.

4 Select a heading style, such as **h1.**

5 Open the **PrintSupport** property group.

6 Change the **page-break-before** option.
You can set the option to always add a page break or to start the heading on the left or right.

To format the TOC and index styles:

1 Open your stylesheet.
Stylesheets are stored in the Resources folder in the Content Explorer.

2 Select the **Print** medium.

3 Click the plus sign beside the **p** style.

4 Select a TOC or index class.

5 Modify the style's properties. The TOC/index-specific style properties include:

Property	Description
mc-leader-indent	Sets the distance between the end of the TOC or index entry and the start of the leader
mc-leader-offset	Sets the distance between the end of the leader and the page number
mc-multiline-indent	Specifies additional indentation for TOC or index entries that wrap to more than one line
mc-pagenum-display	Specifies whether a TOC level should display a page number. If the value is 'leaf,' the page number will not appear if the TOC entry contains sub-entries.
mc-reference-initial-separator	Specifies the text that appears after index entries and before page numbers. The default is ', '
mc-reference-separator	Specifies the text that appears between nonconsecutive page numbers. The default is ', '. For consecutive page numbers, Flare will automatically use a dash.

To use the print medium in a target:

1 Open a target.

2 Select the **Advanced** tab.

3 In the **Stylesheet Medium** field, select **print**.

Adding a medium

You can add a medium to a stylesheet to add target-specific formatting. For example, WebHelp Mobile targets are automatically set up to use the 'mobile' medium.

To add a medium:

1 Open your stylesheet.
   Stylesheets are stored in the Resources folder in the Content Explorer.

2 In the Stylesheet Editor toolbar, click **Options**.

3 Select **Add Medium**.

4 Type a name for the medium.

5 Click **OK**.

Adding a comment to a style NEW!

You can add a comment to a styles to document how and/or when it should be used.

To add a comment to a style:

1 Open your stylesheet.

2 If you are using the Simplified View:

   □ Select a style.

   □ Double-click in the Comment cell.

   □ Type the comment.

   If you are using the Advanced View:

   □ Select a style.

   □ Click in the Comment box below the list of styles.

   □ Type the comment.

Applying a stylesheet to a topic

Most projects use the same stylesheet for every topic. However, you can create multiple stylesheets and associate different stylesheets with specific topics.

Shortcut	Tool Strip	Ribbon
F4 or Ctrl+Shift+P	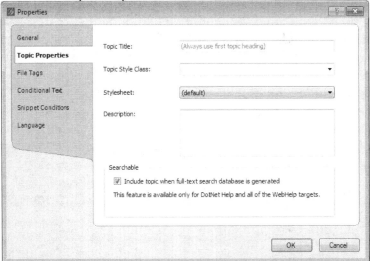 (Content Explorer)	Home > Properties

To assign a stylesheet to a topic:

1 Select a topic and click 🖼.
   —OR—
   Right-click a topic and select **Properties**.

2 Select the **Topic Properties** tab.

3 Select a stylesheet.

4 Click **OK**.
   The stylesheet is applied to the topic.

Applying a stylesheet to multiple topics

You probably don't want to individually associate each topic with your stylesheet. That could take a *long* time! If you want to use multiple stylesheets in a project, you can associate multiple topics with a stylesheet at the same time using the File List.

◇ *If you want to use the same stylesheet for every topic, see 'Applying a stylesheet to all topics' on page 204.*

To apply a stylesheet to multiple topics:

1 Open the File List.
   If the File List is not open, select **View** > **File List**.

2 Filter the File List by **Topic Files**.

3 Select the topics.

4 Right-click the selected topics and select **Properties**.
   The Properties dialog box appears.

5 Select the **Topic Properties** tab.

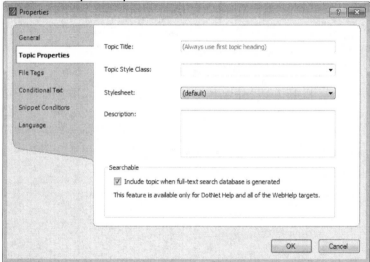

6 Select a **Stylesheet**.

7 Click **OK**.
   The topics are associated with the stylesheet.

Applying a stylesheet to all topics

If you assign a master stylesheet to a project, every topic is
automatically associated with the master stylesheet, including
imported topics and any new topics you create in the future.

Shortcut	Tool Strip	Ribbon
Alt+P, R	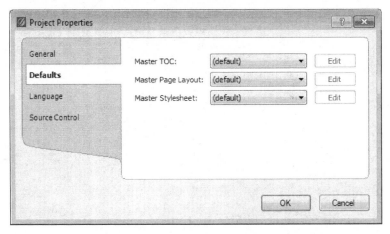 (Project toolbar)	Home > Project Properties

To apply a stylesheet to all topics:

1 Select **Project** > **Project Properties**.
The Project Properties dialog box appears.

2 On the **General** tab, select a **Master Stylesheet**.

3 Click **OK**.

Master pages

You can create a master page to include content at the top or bottom of topics in online targets, such as WebHelp. In addition to text, images, tables and other content, you can include the following dynamic elements (Flare calls these elements 'proxies') in a master page:

- **Breadcrumbs** automatically provide a list of the TOC books above the current topic. If your books are linked to topics, the books in the breadcrumb path are also linked.

- A **mini-TOC** automatically adds a list of links to 'book-level' topics in your TOC. For example, if a TOC book links to the 'Overview' topic and the book contains pages that link to topics A, B, and C, a mini-TOC would add links to topics A, B, and C to the Overview topic.

'Is a master page the same as a RoboHelp template?'

Flare's master pages are very similar to RoboHelp's templates. However, Flare converts headers and footers in RoboHelp templates to snippets and insert the snippets into the topics that used the template. A snippet is content that you can reuse in your topics—not just in the header or footer. For more information about snippets, see page 240.

Creating a master page

You can create as many master pages as you need. Master pages have a .flmsp extension, and they are stored in the Resources\MasterPages folder in the Content Explorer.

Shortcut	Tool Strip	Ribbon
Ctrl+T	▣ (Content Explorer)	File > New

To create a master page:

1 Select **File** > **New**.
The Add File dialog box appears.

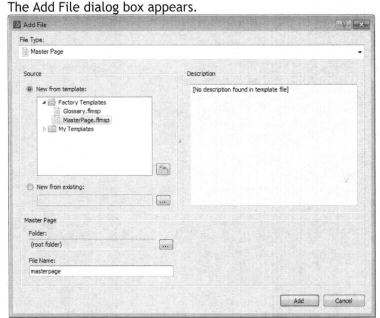

2 For **File Type**, select **Master Page**.

3 Select a **Source** template.

4 Type a **File name**.
Master pages have a .flmsp extension. If you don't type the extension, Flare will add it for you.

5 Click **Add**.
The Copy to Project dialog box appears.

6 Click **OK**.
The master page appears in the Content Explorer and opens in the XML Editor.

Adding content to a master page

You can add content to a master page above or below the topic body proxy.

Any content that you add above the topic body proxy will appear above the topic's content. However, it is not 'fixed' on the screen: it will scroll off the page in long topics.

Any content that you add below the topic body proxy will appear at the bottom of the topic. In long topics, users may need to scroll down to see it.

To add content to a master page:

1 Open the master page.

2 Position the cursor above or below the **topic body** proxy.

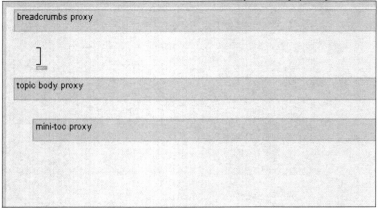

3 Type or insert your header's content.
You can add anything to a master page that you can add to a topic, including formatted content, images, lists, tables, variables, and snippets.

To add a proxy to a master page:

1 Open the master page.

2 Position the cursor above or below the **topic body** proxy.

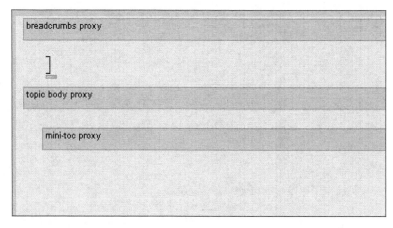

3   Select **Insert** > **Proxy** and select a proxy.

Applying a master page to a target

To use a master page, you need to associate it with a target. You can associate the same master page with multiple targets, or you can associate a different master page with each of your targets.

To apply a master page to a target:

1   Open a target.

2   Select the **Advanced** tab.

3   Select a **Master Page**.

4   Click **Save**.

Page layouts

You can create a page layout to set the page size and margins and to add headers and footers to print targets. You can add pages to a page layout to set up different headers and footers for first, title, left, and odd pages.

Creating a page layout

You can create multiple page layouts to apply different page sizes, margins, headers, or footers to different sections in a print target. For example, you can create a landscape page layout for wide tables or large graphics.

Page layouts have a .flpgl extension, and they are stored in the Resources\PageLayouts folder in the Content Explorer.

To create a page layout:

1 Select **File** > **New**.
The Add File dialog box appears.

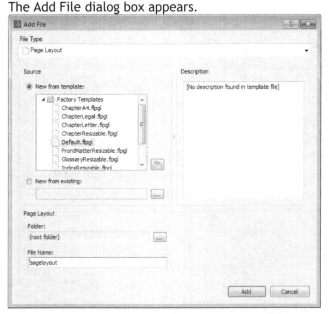

2 For **File Type**, select **Page Layout**.

3 Select a **Source** template.

4 Type a **File Name**.

5 Click **Add**.
   The page layout appears in the Page Layout Editor.

Adding pages to a page layout

You can include the following types of pages in a page layout:

Page Type	Description
Title	The title page is often used for a cover or title page, which is also usually the first page in your TOC.
First First Left First Right	The first page is often used for the first page in a chapter. For more information about adding chapter breaks, see 'Specifying chapter breaks' on page 155.
Left	The left page is automatically used for the left (even) pages.
Right	The right page is automatically used for the right (odd) pages.
Empty Empty Left Empty Right	Empty pages are inserted as needed if you set up chapters to end on left pages or set up styles (such as headings) to start on left or right pages. If you do not have an empty page in your page layout, the inserted page will be blank.

TIP *If you are creating left and right pages for a Word target, you should also select the "Generate 'Mirror Margins' for MS Word Output" option on the Advanced tab in your Word target.*

To add a page to a page layout:

1 Open a page layout.

2 In the Page Layout Editor toolbar, click 📄 and select **Add Page**.
   The new page appears.

3 Right-click the page and select **Page Properties**.
The Page Properties dialog box appears.

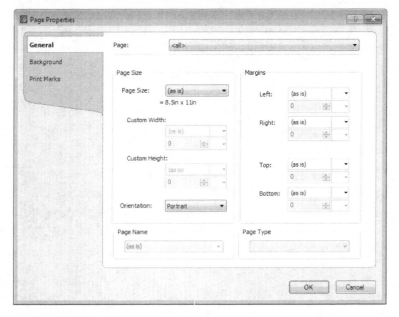

4 Select a **Page Type**.

5 Type a **Page Name**.

6 Click **OK**.

Duplicating a page

Instead of adding pages, you can duplicate a page in a page layout. If you add a page, you will need to add and set up the frames in the page. Duplicate a page is usually easier, since the frames are already set up.

To duplicate a page:

1 Open a page layout.

2 Right-click a page icon and select **Duplicate Page**.

3 Set up the new page.

Adding a frame to a page layout

You can add a decoration or image frame to include text or images on a page. For example, you can add a decoration frame to include the word "draft" on a page.

To add a decoration frame to a page layout:

1 Open a page layout.

2 Select a page.

3 Click .

4 Select **New Decoration Frame Mode**.
   The cursor changes to a crosshair.

5 Click and drag to draw the decoration frame.

6 Right-click inside the decoration frame and select **Edit Text**.

7 If you want to use a template, select **Yes** and select a template.

8 Add content to the frame.
   You can include any type of content in the frame, including text, images, tables, snippets, and variables.

To add an image frame to a page layout:

1 Open a page layout.

2 Select a page.

3 Click .

4 Select **New Image Frame**.
   The Insert Image dialog box appears.

5 Select an image.

6 Position the image frame on the page.

Adding running headings to a header or footer

You can use Flare's built-in heading variables to add running headings to a header or footer. A 'running' header variable automatically updates whenever the specified heading level appears. For example, the footer in each chapter of this book automatically changes for each heading level 1.

To add a running heading to a header or footer:

1 Open a page layout.

2 Right-click a header or footer and select **Edit Text**.
The header or footer pane appears.

3 Select **Insert > Variable**.

4 In the **Variable Sets** column, select **Heading**.

5 Select one of the 'Level' variables.
The level1-6 variables match the h1-h6 styles.

6 Click **OK**.

Adding page numbers to a header or footer

You can use Flare's built-in system variables to add page numbers to a header or footer.

To add page numbers to a header or footer:

1 Open a page layout.

2 Right-click a header or footer and select **Edit Text**.
The header or footer pane appears.

3 Select **Insert > Variable**.

4 In the **Variable Sets** column, select **System**.

5 Select the **PageNumber** variable.

> **TIP** *You can use the **PageCount** variable to insert the total page count.*

6 Click **OK**.

Creating a two-column page layout

You can add another body frame to a page layout to create a two column page layout.

To create a two-column page layout:

1 Open a page layout.

2 Select a page.

3 Select the **body** frame.

4 Size the body frame to make space for the second column.

5 Right-click the body frame and select **Copy**.

6 Right-click the body frame again and select **Paste**.

7 Position the new body frame. You will see an arrow between the two body frames that indicates how the content will flow between the frames.

Rotating frames in a page layout

You can rotate a frame clockwise or counter clockwise in 45 degree increments.

To rotate a frame:

1 Open a page layout.

2 Select a page.

3 Select a frame.

4 Click **Layout**.

5 Select **Rotate** and select a **Rotation** option.

Stacking frames in a page layout

If your frames overlap, you can set their stacking order by moving them above or below each other.

To move a frame below or above another frame:

1 Open a page layout.

2 Select a page.

3 Select a frame.

4 Click **Layout**.

5 Select **Depth** and select a whether the frame should move above (float) or below (sink) other overlapping frames.

Applying a page layout to a topic

To assign a page type to a topic, you need to add a chapter or page layout break in your TOC.

To add a break in a TOC:

1 Open a TOC.

2 Right-click a TOC book or page and select **Properties**. The Properties dialog box appears.

3 Select the **Printed Output** tab.

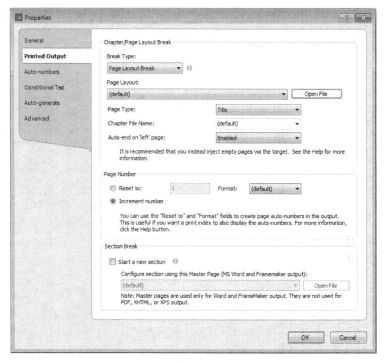

4 For **Break Type**, select **Chapter Break or Page Layout Break**.
   If you want to restart the page numbering or change the page
   number format, select **Chapter Break**. If not, select **Page
   Layout Break**.

5 Select a **Page Layout**.

6 Select a **Page Type**.

7 Select whether you want the chapter to **Auto-end on 'left'**
   page.

8 Click **OK**.

Applying a page layout to a target

1 Open a target.

2 On the **General** tab, select a **Master Page Layout**.

Skins

Skins are used to format the toolbar and navigation pane and to set the size of the window for online targets. The WebHelp formats support the most customization options, followed by DotNet Help and HTML Help.

Skin files have a .flskn extension. They appear in the Skins folder in the Project Organizer.

'Is there a skin gallery?'

You can download and customize skins from MadCap's website at www.madcapsoftware.com/downloads/flareskingallery.aspx.

Creating a skin

You can use the same skin for all of your online targets, or you can create different skins for each target.

Shortcut	Tool Strip	Ribbon
Ctrl+T	▦ (Content Explorer)	File > New

To create a skin:

1   Select **File** > **New**.
    —OR—
    Right-click the **Skins** folder and select **Add Skin**.
    The Add File dialog box appears.

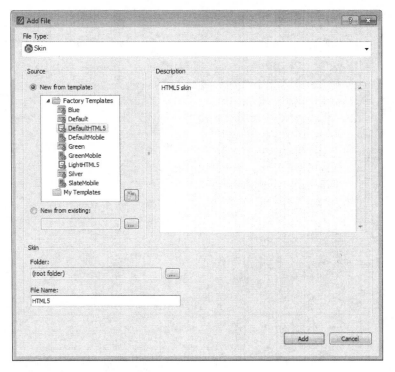

2   For **File Type**, select **Skin**.

3   Select a **Source** template.

4   Type a **File Name**.
    Skins have a .flskn extension. If you don't type the extension,
    Flare will add it for you.

5   Click **Add**.
    The Copy to Project dialog box appears.

6   Click **OK**.
    The skin appears in the Skins folder in the Project Organizer
    and opens in the Skin Editor.

Modifying an HTML5 skin NEW!

You can modify a skin to change the size, appearance, and features
used in your HTML5 targets.

To modify an HTML5 skin:

1 Open the skin.

The skin appears in the HTML5 Skin Editor.

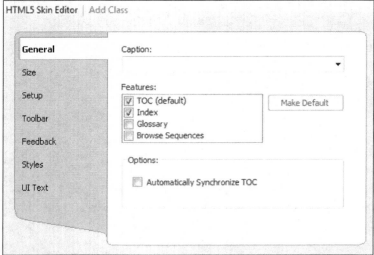

2 On the **General** tab, type a **Caption**.

The caption appears in the browser's title bar or tab.

3 Select the **Features** that you want to appear in the help window.

4 Enable or disable **Automatically Synchronize TOC**.

5 Select the **Size** tab.

6 If you want to specify a size for your help window:

☐ Deselect **Use Browser Default Size**.

☐ Type values for the window positions.
—OR—
Click **Preview Full Size**, resize the preview window, and click **OK**.

7 Select the **Setup** tab.

☐ Select a **Pane Position**.

☐ Type a **Pane Size**.

□ If you want your content to resize and adapt to different screen sizes, select **Enable responsive output**.

8 Select the **Toolbar** tab.

□ Select the **Toolbar Buttons** you want to include:

Button	Description
Current Topic Index	The current topic's position in the browse sequence. For example, 'Page 2 of 5.'
Edit User Profile	Opens the Feedback Service Profile dialog box.
Expand All	Expands (or collapses) all toggler, drop-down, and expanding links in the current topic.
Filler	Adds space between buttons
Next Topic	Opens the next topic in the browse sequence.
Previous Topic	Opens the previous topic in the browse sequence.
Print	Open the Print dialog box.
Separator	Adds a dividing line between buttons.
Topic Ratings	Shows the topic rating icons (stars by default) that can be used to rate a topic

8 Select the **Styles** tab and modify the styles as needed. You can change fonts, icons, labels, borders, paddings, and background settings and other style properties for the skin elements.

TIP▶ *To change or remove the MadCap logo, open the **Header** style group, select **Logo**, select **Background**, and change the **Image** setting.*

9 Select the **UI Text** tab and modify any of the labels or tooltips.

10 Click **Save**.

Modifying a WebHelp, DotNet Help, and HTML Help skin

You can modify a skin to change the size, appearance, and features used in your WebHelp, DotNet Help, and HTML Help targets.

To modify a skin:

1 Open the skin.
The skin appears in the Skin Editor.

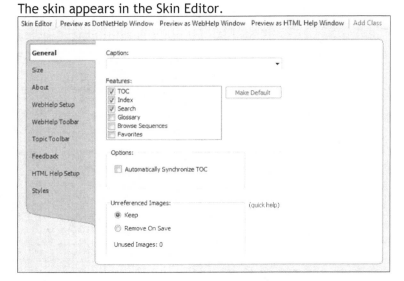

2 On the **General** tab, type a **Caption**.
The caption appears in the browser window's title bar or tab.

3 Select the **Features** that you want to appear in the help window.

4 Enable or disable **Automatically Synchronize TOC**.

5 Select the **Size** tab.

6 If you want to specify a size for your help window:

☐ Deselect **Use Browser Default Size**.

□ Type values for the window positions.

—OR—

Click **Preview Full Size**, resize the preview window, and click **OK**.

7 If you are editing a WebHelp skin:

□ Select the **About** tab.

□ Select an **About** box image.
The About box appears when the user clicks the logo on the far right of the toolbar.

□ Select the **WebHelp Setup** tab.

□ Select a **Pane Position**.

□ Type a **Navigation Pane Size**.

□ Select the number of **Visible Accordion Items** you would like to use (navigational features appear in an 'accordion,' similar to tabs). If you have selected more navigational features on the **General** tab than visible accordion items, the additional items will appear as icons below the accordion.

□ Select the **WebHelp Toolbar** tab.

□ Select the **Toolbar Buttons** you want to include:

Button	Description
Add Topic to Favorites	Adds the current topic to the Favorites list.
Back	Opens the previously-viewed topic.
Collapse All	Collapses all toggler, drop-down, and expanding links in the current topic.
Current Topic Index	The current topic's position in the browse sequence. For example, 'Page 2 of 5.'
Edit User Profile	Opens the Feedback Service Profile dialog box.
Expand All	Expands all toggler, drop-down, and expanding links in the current topic.

Button	Description
Forward	Opens the next topic (if the user has previously clicked the Back button).
Home	Opens the startup topic as specified on the Target's General tab.
Next Topic	Opens the next topic in the browse sequence.
Previous Topic	Opens the previous topic in the browse sequence.
Print	Open the Print dialog box.
Quick Search	Searches the current topic for a word or phrase.
Refresh	Reopens the current topic.
Remove Highlight	Turns off search highlighting.
Select Browse Sequence	Open the browse sequence in the navigation pane.
Select Favorites	Open the favorites list in the navigation pane.
Select Glossary	Opens the glossary in the navigation pane.
Select Index	Opens the index in the navigation pane.
Select Search	Opens the search in the navigation pane.
Select TOC	Opens table of contents in the navigation pane.
Separator	Adds a dividing line between buttons.
Stop	Cancels opening the topic.
Toggle Navigation Pane	Hides and shows the navigation pane.
Topic Ratings	Shows the topic rating icons (stars by default) that can be used to rate a topic.

8 If you are editing an HTML Help skin:

☐ Click the **HTML Help Setup** tab.

☐ Select the **HTML Help Buttons** you want to include:

Button	Description
Hide	Hides and shows the navigation pane.
Locate	Highlights the current topic in the TOC.
Back	Opens the previously-viewed topic.
Forward	Opens the next topic (if the user has previously clicked the Back button).
Stop	Cancels opening the topic.
Refresh	Reopens the current topic.
Home	Opens the startup topic as specified on the Target's General tab.
Font	Increases the font size in topics.
Print	Open the Print dialog box.
QuickSearch	Searches the current topic.
Next	Opens the next topic in the TOC.
Previous	Opens the previous topic in the TOC.
Options	Opens a menu with the following commands: Home, Show, Back, Stop, Refresh, and Search Highlight On/Off.
Jump 1 and 2	Opens a specified website or topic (click Jump Button Options to select a target).

☐ Select the **Button, Navigation Pane,** and **Misc Options** you want to use.

TIP▶ *To include the WebHelp toolbar (created on the WebHelp Toolbar tab) in HTML Help, select Display Toolbar in Each Topic.*

9 If you are editing a WebHelp skin, select the **Styles** tab and modify the styles as needed. You can change the font, icon, label, border, padding, and background settings for any toolbar item.

TIP▷ *To change or remove the MadCap logo, open the* ***Toolbarltem*** *style group, select* ***Logo***, *and change the* ***Icon*** *setting.*

10 Click **Save**.

Modifying a WebHelp mobile skin

You can modify a WebHelp mobile skin to change the 'about' image, toolbar buttons, and appearance used in your mobile targets.

To modify a WebHelp mobile skin:

1 Open the skin.
The skin appears in the WebHelp Mobile Skin Editor.

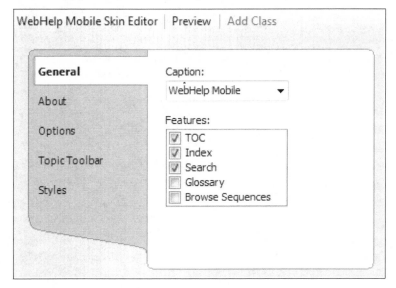

2 On the **General** tab, type a **Caption**.
The caption appears in the browser's title bar or tab.

3 Select the **Features** that you want to appear in the help window.

4   Select the **About** tab and select an **About Box Bitmap** image. The About box appears when the user clicks the logo on the far right of the toolbar.

5   Select the **Options** tab and select whether you want to display the number of sub-items inside a TOC or browse sequence book or the number of linked topics for an index entry.

6   Select the **Topic Toolbar** tab and select the **Toolbar Buttons** you want to include:

Button	Description
Collapse All	Collapses all toggler, drop-down, and expanding links in the current topic.
CurrentTopicIndex	The current topic's position in the browse sequence. For example, 'Page 2 of 5.'
Expand All	Expands all toggler, drop-down, and expanding links in the current topic.
NextTopic	Opens the next topic in the browse sequence.
PreviousTopic	Opens the previous topic in the browse sequence.

7   Select the **Styles** tab and modify the styles as needed. You can change the font, icon, label, border, padding, and background settings for any toolbar item.

8   Click **Save**.

Applying a skin with a target

To use a skin, you need to associate it with a target. You can associate the same skin with multiple targets, or you can associate different skins with each target.

To associate a skin with a target:

1   Open a target.

2   On the **General** tab, select a **Skin**.

3   Click **Save**.

Responsive output NEW!

Rather than creating, designing, building, and publishing a WebHelp Mobile and WebHelp or HTML5 target, you can enable responsive output in an HTML5 target. The responsive output option allows your HTML5 target to automatically change when it is viewed on a regular PC, a tablet, or a phone. So, you would only need one target instead of two. Since the output would automatically adjust, you also would not need to add code to detect the user's device.

Enabling responsive output

You can enable responsive output in an HTML5 skin.

To enable responsive output:

1 Double-click an HTML5 skin.
  The HTML5 Skin Editor appears.

2 Select the **Setup** tab.

3 Select **Enable Responsive Output**.

4 If you want to change the maximum width settings for tablets or mobile devices, type a size.

Designing responsive output

You can use the Web, Tablet, and Mobile mediums in an HTML5 skin to specify how your content will appear on each type of device.

To design responsive output:

1 Double-click an HTML5 skin.
  The HTML5 Skin Editor appears.

2 Select the **Styles** tab.

3 In the HTML5 Skin Editor toolbar, click **Web Medium**.

4 Set the colors, icons, fonts, and other settings for the web medium. The web medium will be used when your content is viewed on a PC.

5 Click **Table Medium**.
The Tablet medium inherits all of the settings from the Web medium. The only elements that are automatically different are the navigation icons since they are different sizes.

6 Set any design elements that should be different in the tablet medium.

7 Click **Mobile Medium**.
The Mobile medium inherits all of the settings from the Tablet medium. The only elements that are automatically different are the navigation icons since they are different sizes.

8 Set any design elements that should be different in the mobile medium.

Viewing responsive output

After you build an HTML5 target, you can view it as it will appear on a tablet or phone.

To view responsive output:

1 Build an HTML5 target.

2 In the Build Progress dialog box, click View Output.

3 Select **Smartphone** or **Tablet**.
The content appears in a preview window that looks like the selected device.

When you view the HTML5 target using the Smartphone or Tablet option, it does not open in an emulator. Instead, it opens in your browser inside a picture of a tablet or phone. You can use these views to review the design, but they are not for testing. To test your content, you should open it using a tablet and/or phone or use an emulator. You can download emulators at the following websites:

Android — developer.android.com/sdk/index.html

iOS — developer.apple.com/devcenter/ios/index.action

Windows Phone — msdn.microsoft.com/en-us/library/windowsphone/
develop/ff402563%28v=vs.105%29.aspx

Sample questions for this section

1 What is inline formatting?
A) Formatting that is applied to a word or phrase rather than an entire block of content.
B) Formatting that is applied by highlighting content and changing its appearance.
C) 'Track changes' lines that automatically appear for new or modified content.
D) Formatting that applies a strikethrough line to your content.

2 You should consider using a font set if you plan to create which format?
A) HTML Help
B) DotNet Help
C) WebHelp
D) PDF

3 If you select a master stylesheet, it is automatically assigned to which topics?
A) Existing topics
B) Imported topics
C) New topics you create after selecting the master stylesheet
D) All of the above

4 What is a breadcrumb?
A) The path to the current topic using the TOC.
B) The list of previous topics the user has viewed.
C) A way to mark a topic, like a favorite, so that it can be quickly found again.
D) A user comment about a topic.

5 How can you set different odd and even footers for a print target?
A) Create two master pages.
B) Create two page layouts.
C) Create a template with two master pages.
D) Create an odd and even page in a page layout.

6 Your skin includes 6 accordion items, but 'Visible Accordion Items' is set to 4. Where do the other 2 accordion items appear in your WebHelp target?

A) They don't appear.

B) They all appear as accordion items.

C) They appear as icons below the accordion.

D) WebHelp uses tabs, not accordion items.

7 How do you apply a skin to a target?

A) Open the skin and select the target on the **Targets** tab.

B) Open the target and select the skin in the **General** tab.

C) Open the target and select the skin on the **Skins** tab.

D) Select **Project Properties** and select the skin as the **Master Skin**.

Single source

This section covers:

- Variables
- Snippets
- Condition tags

Variables

A variable can only contain unformatted text. I often use variables for copyright statements and product names. If the copyright statement or product name changes, I just change my variable's definition and all of my topics are updated.

Flare also provides dynamic system and heading variables. System variables can be used to insert the date, time, page count, page number, and topic title. Heading variables can be used to insert the current heading (any level or a specific level). System and heading variables are often used in page layouts to set up headers and footers for print targets.

User-defined variables are stored in a variable set. You can create as many variable sets and variables as you need. Variable sets are stored in a file with a .flvar extension. They appear in the Variables folder in the Project Organizer.

In older versions of Flare, you had to manually reinsert a variable if you changed its name. Flare 8 and later automatically update the variable's name throughout your project.

Creating a variable set

You can create multiple variable sets to organize your variables or to share company-wide variables between projects.

Shortcut	Tool Strip	Ribbon
Ctrl+T	(Content Explorer)	File > New

To create a variable set:

1 Select **File** > **New**.
 —OR—
 Right-click the **Variables** folder and select **Add Variable Set**. The Add File dialog box appears.

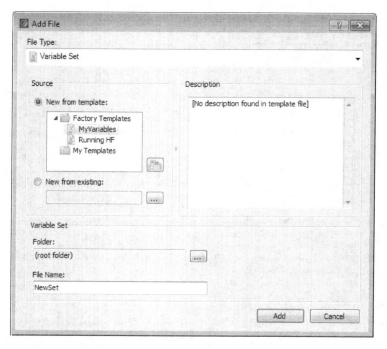

2   For **File Type**, select **Variable Set**.

3   Select a **Source** template.

4   Type a **File Name**.

5   Click **Add**.

Creating a variable NEW!

You can create as many variables as you need. In Flare V

10, you can assign multiple definitions to a variable.

To create a variable:

1   Double-click a variable set.
    The Variable Set Editor window appears.

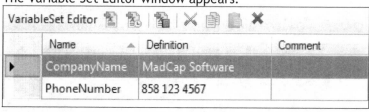

2 Click 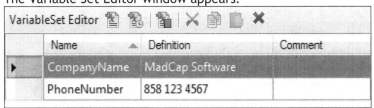 in the Variable Set Editor toolbar.

3 Type a name for the variable.

4 Type a definition for the variable.

5 If you want to add another definition:

□ Click 📑.

□ Type the definition.

Creating a date/time variable NEW!

You can create a date/time variable to insert the date and/or time using one of Microsoft's date and time formats. For more information about Microsoft's date and time formats, see msdn.microsoft.com/en-us/library/8kb3ddd4.aspx

To create a date/time variable:

1 Double-click a variable set.
The Variable Set Editor window appears.

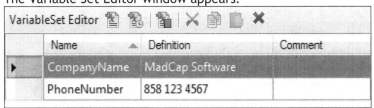

2 Click 📑 in the Variable Set Editor toolbar.

3 Type a name for the variable.

4 Click inside the definition cell.
The Edit Format dialog box appears.

5 Type a date/time format.
For example: ddd MM/dd/yy could appear as Sun 03/30/69

Inserting a variable

You can insert a variable into a topic, snippet, master page, or page layout.

Shortcut	Tool Strip	Ribbon
Ctrl+Shift+V	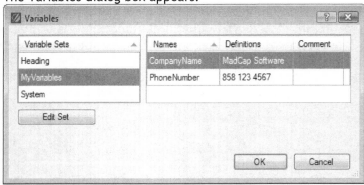 (XML Editor)	Insert > Variable

To insert a variable:

1 Place your cursor where you want to insert the variable.

2 Select **Insert** > **Variable**.
The Variables dialog box appears.

3 Select a variable set.

4 Select a variable.

5 Click **OK**.
The variable appears in the topic.

TIP *You can also drag a variable from the Project Organizer into a topic.*

Overriding a variable's definition in a target

You can specify a variable's definition when you create a target. Flare will then use the selected definition wherever you inserted the variable in your project.

To override a variable's definition:

1 Open the target.

2 Select the **Variables** tab.

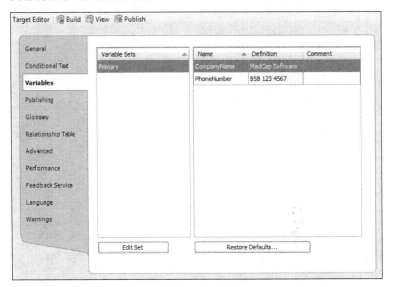

3 Click the variable's **Definition** cell and type a value. If you added multiple definitions when you created the variable, you can select a definition from the list.

Snippets

A snippet can include any type of content, including formatted text, links, images, tables, lists, and variables. I often create snippets for tables and steps that I need to use in multiple topics.

Snippets are stored in a file with a .flsnp extension. They appear in the Resources\Snippets folder in the Content Explorer.

Creating a snippet using existing content

You can select content within a topic and convert it to a snippet.

Shortcut	Tool Strip	Ribbon
Alt+H, S, P	Format > Create Snippet	Home > Create Snippet

To create a snippet using existing content:

1   Open the topic that contains the content you want to convert to a snippet.

2   Highlight the content you want to convert to a snippet.

3   Select **Home** > **Create Snippet**.
    The Create Snippet dialog box appears.

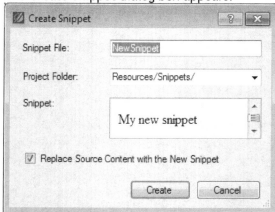

4   In the **Snippet File** field, type a new name for the snippet.

5 Leave the project folder selection as **Resources/Snippets**.

6 If you want the snippet to replace the highlighted text in the topic, select the **Replace Source Content with the New Snippet** option.

7 Click **Create**.
The snippet is created.

Creating a snippet using new content

You can also create a blank snippet and add content to it.

Shortcut	Tool Strip	Ribbon
Ctrl+T	▤ (Content Explorer)	File > New

To create a snippet using new content:

1 Select **File** > **New**.
The Add File dialog box appears.

2 For **File Type**, select **Snippet**.

3 Select a **Source** template.

4 Select a **Folder**.
By default, snippets are stored in the Resources/Snippets folder.

5 Type a **File Name** for the snippet.

6 Click **Add**.
The Copy to Project dialog box appears.

7 Click **OK**.
The snippet appears in Content Explorer and opens in the XML Editor.

8 Click inside the snippet page in the XML Editor and add your content.

Inserting a snippet

You can insert snippets into topics, master pages, and page layouts.

Shortcut	Tool Strip	Ribbon
Ctrl+R	(XML Editor)	Insert > Snippet

To insert a snippet to a topic:

1 Position the cursor where you want to insert the snippet.

2 Select **Insert > Snippet**.
The Insert Snippet Link dialog box appears.

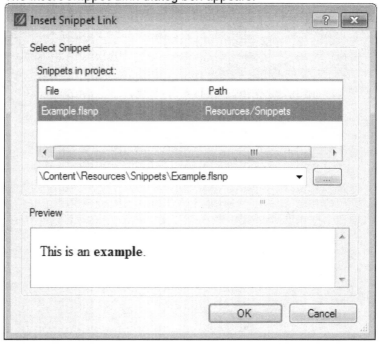

3 Select a snippet.
A preview of the snippet appears.

4 Click **OK**.
The snippet is added to the topic.

Condition tags

Condition tags can be used to exclude content when you create an online or print target. For example, you could create an 'InternalOnly' tag and exclude it when you create a knowledgebase for customers.

You can apply a condition tag to almost anything: folders, topics, content in topics, TOC entries, index entries, stylesheets, variables, and snippets. Flare also makes it easier to specify which tags you want to include and exclude when you create a target.

Condition tags are stored in a condition tag set. When you import a RoboHelp project or FrameMaker document that contains conditional build tags, your tags are stored in a condition tag named after your import file.

TIP> *If you insert an image created with MadCap Capture or insert a video created with MadCap Mimic into a Flare project, you can use your Flare project's condition tags in the image or video.*

Conditional tag sets have a .flcts extension. They appear in the Conditional Text folder in the Project Organizer.

'What are those boxes in the Content Explorer?'

They're called 'condition tag boxes.'

When you create a condition tag, you assign a color to the tag. This color is used to identify tagged content in a topic. If a folder or topic is associated with a tag, the condition tag box is filled with the tag's assigned color. If the folder or topic is associated with multiple tags, the condition tag box uses vertical stripes to show each tag's color.

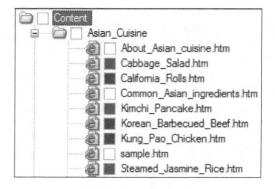

Creating a condition tag

Shortcut	Tool Strip	Ribbon
Ctrl+T	▦ (Content Explorer)	File > New

To create a condition tag:

1 Open the Project Organizer.

2 Open the **Conditional Text** folder.

3 Double-click a condition tag set.
The Condition Tag Set Editor appears.

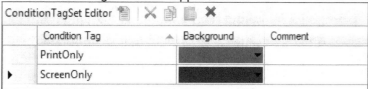

4 Click ▤ in the Condition Tag Set Editor toolbar.
A new tag appears.

5 Double-click the new tag's name.

6 Type a new name for the tag and press **Enter**.

7 Select a color.

In older versions of Flare, you had to reapply a tag if you changed its name. Flare 8 and later automatically update the condition tag's name throughout your project.

Applying a tag to content in a topic

To apply a tag to content in a topic:

1   Open a topic.

2   Select the content to be tagged.
    You can apply a tag to any content, including characters, words, paragraphs, table columns/rows, items in a list, and images.

3   Select **Home** > **Conditions**.
    —OR—
    Press Ctrl+Shift+C.
    The Condition Tags dialog box appears.

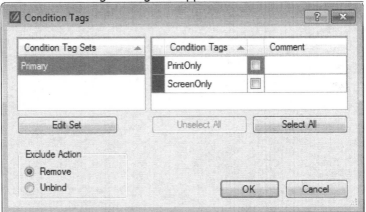

4   Select a condition tag's checkbox.

5   Click **OK**.
    The tag is applied. The tagged content is shaded using the tag's color.

Applying a tag to a topic, file, or folder

To apply a tag to a topic, file, or folder:

1 Open the Content Explorer.

2 Select the topic, file, or folder to be tagged.

3 Click 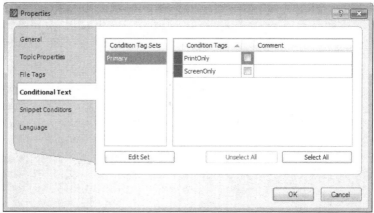 in the Content Explorer toolbar.
The Properties dialog box appears.

4 Select the **Conditional Text** tab.

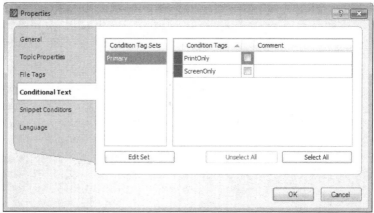

5 Select a condition tag's checkbox.

6 Click **OK**.
The tag is applied and the file or folder's condition tag box is filled with the tag's color.

Applying a tag to a TOC book or page

You can also apply a condition tag to a TOC book or page instead of a topic. For online targets, excluding a tagged TOC item only removes it from the TOC. Excluding a tagged topic removes the topic from the TOC, index, and search.

To apply a tag to a TOC book or page:

1 Open the Project Organizer.

2 Double-click a TOC.

3   Select a book or page and click 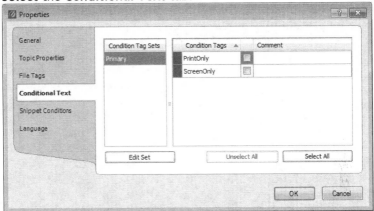 in the TOC Editor.
The Properties dialog box appears.

4   Select the **Conditional Text** tab.

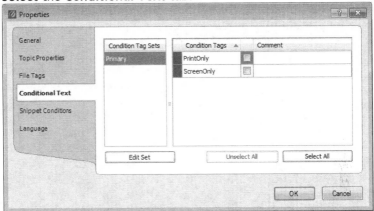

5   Select a condition tag's checkbox.

6   Click **OK**.
The tag is applied and the TOC book or page's condition tag box is filled with the tag's color.

Applying a tag to an index entry

To apply a tag to an index entry:

1   Open a topic.

2   Select an index entry marker.

3 Select **Home** > **Conditions.**
The Condition Tags dialog box appears.

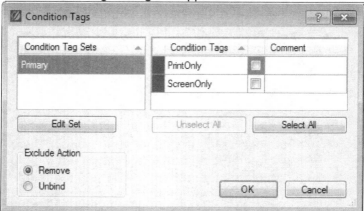

4 Select a condition tag's checkbox.

5 Click **OK.**
The tag is applied. A condition tag box appears inside the tagged index entry's marker.

Including or excluding a tag when you build a target

By default, all of your content is included when you build a target. In fact, tagged content is also included unless you exclude it.

For example, a project might contain a two condition tags: A and B. Some content is tagged as A, some content is tagged as B, and some content is tagged as A and B.

You could use a basic build expression to:

□   exclude A

□   exclude B

□   include content tagged as A,
include content tagged as A and B, and
exclude content tagged only as B

☐ include content tagged as B,
include content tagged as A and B, and
exclude content tagged only as A

However, you would need to use an advanced build expression to include content tagged as A and B but <u>exclude</u> content that is tagged as only A or B. This build expression would be written as:

(myTags.A and myTags.B) or not (myTags.A or myTags.B)

To include or exclude a tag when you build a target (basic):

1 Open a target.

2 Select the **Conditional Text** tab.

3 Select **Basic**.

4 Select the tags you want to **Exclude**.

5 If you have assigned more than one tag to topics or blocks on content in topics, select the tags you want to **Include**.

6 Save the target.

To create an advanced build expression (advanced):

1 Open a target.

2 Select the **Conditional Text** tab.

3 Select **Advanced**.

4 In the **Advanced** text box, type a build expression.

5 Save the target.

Sample questions for this section

1 Where are variables stored?
   A) In variable sets in the Project Organizer
   B) In variable files in the Content Explorer's Resources folder
   C) In variable files in the Content Explorer's Variables folder
   D) Inside topics

2 A variable's definition can be set: (select all that apply)
   A) Inside a topic
   B) In the VariableSet Editor
   C) In a target on the Variables tab
   D) In the Project Properties on the Variables tab

3 A snippet can contain: (select all that apply)
   A) Formatted text
   B) Tables
   C) Lists
   D) Variables

4 Where are snippets are stored?
   A) In snippet sets in the Project Organizer
   B) In snippet files in the Project Organizer
   C) In snippet files in the Content Explorer
   D) Inside topics

5 A condition tag can be applied to: (select all that apply)
   A) Topics
   B) Folders
   C) TOC books and pages
   D) Index keywords

6 What happens if you rename a condition tag after it has been applied
   to content?
   A) Flare automatically updates the content to use the new condition
   tag name.
   B) Flare asks if you want to update the content to use the new name.
   C) The condition tag is removed from your content.
   D) Nothing—you must update the content yourself to use the new
   name.

7 Condition tags can be applied to the following targets:
A) PDF
B) Word
C) HTML Help
D) Any type of target

Build and publish

This section covers:

- Targets
- Context-sensitive help

Targets

You can create sixteen types of online and print targets from Flare. Each target type is summarized in the tables below.

Online targets

Target	Description
DITA	A 'code' format that creates DITA-based topics and a DITA map. These files can be integrated into another application or a content management system ('CMS').
DotNet Help	An online format developed by MadCap Software that can be used to create Windows-based help for .NET applications. DotNet Help runs in the MadCap Help Viewer, and DotNet targets have a .mchelp file extension.
Eclipse Help **NEW!**	An online format that can be used to create an Eclipse Help plug-in that can be viewed in the Eclipse Help viewer.
HTML Help	An online format developed by Microsoft that can be used to create Windows-based help. Microsoft no longer maintains or supports the HTML Help format, and they have promised an eventual replacement. HTML Help targets run in the HTML Help Viewer and they have a .chm (often pronounced 'chum') file extension.
HTML5	An online format developed by MadCap Software that is similar to WebHelp. HTML5 has a different design, and the search results look like Google's.
WebHelp	An online format developed by MadCap Software that can be used to create Web-based content such as help systems. WebHelp runs in a browser, so it is not Windows-specific like DotNet Help and HTML Help.
WebHelp Mobile	A special version of WebHelp that was designed to be viewed on handheld devices such as iPhones.
WebHelp Plus	A special version of WebHelp that provides faster searches and allows users to search content in .pdf, .doc, and .xls files. Unlike WebHelp, WebHelp Plus requires a Microsoft Web server with IIS.

WebHelp AIR   A special version of WebHelp that can be run locally
                rather than from a Web server. WebHelp AIR requires
                Adobe AIR, and WebHelp AIR targets have a .air file
                extension.

'What is DITA?'

DITA stands for 'Darwin Information Typing Architecture.' It was
created by IBM, but it is now a standard of the Organization for the
Advancement of Structured Information Standards (OASIS).

'What is DotNet Help?'

MadCap's DotNet Help is a format that was designed to be used with
.NET applications. It is similar to WebHelp, but it runs inside the freely
distributable MadCap Help viewer.

'What is Eclipse Help?' **NEW!**

Eclipse Help is a new format that can be used to create an Eclipse Help
plug-in. Eclipse Help plug-ins can be viewed in the Eclipse Help viewer.
The Eclipse Help viewer uses an embedded Jetty server to provide
navigational features including a TOC, index, and search. For
information about customizing the Eclipse Help viewer, see
help.eclipse.org/kepler/index.jsp.

'What is HTML5?'

HTML5 is a recommendation from the W3C that was created to replace
HTML and XHTML. HTML5 targets do not use frames, and they have a
more modern design than WebHelp targets.

HTML Help cannot run from a file server because Microsoft has
disabled the format for 'security reasons.'

WebHelp cannot run locally or from a file server in Internet Explorer
because Microsoft blocks 'active content.' Users can enable active
content in Internet Explorer, but you will need to provide instructions.

TIP▶ *To enable active content in Internet Explorer, open Internet
Explorer, select **Tools > Options**, click **Advanced**, and turn on **Allow
active content to run in files on My Computer**.*

'What about WinHelp?'

Flare cannot create WinHelp. Microsoft's WinHelp is an old help format that was replaced by HTML Help in the late 1990s. Microsoft slowly phased out WinHelp over ten years, and they stopped supporting it with Windows Vista.

'Is Flare's WebHelp the same as RoboHelp's WebHelp?'

Flare's version of WebHelp looks very different from RoboHelp's WebHelp. Flare's WebHelp uses an accordion to display the TOC, index, search, and glossary.

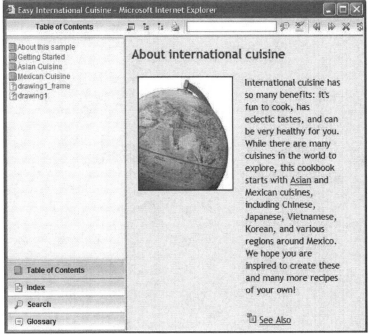

Flare's WebHelp

Flare's HTML5

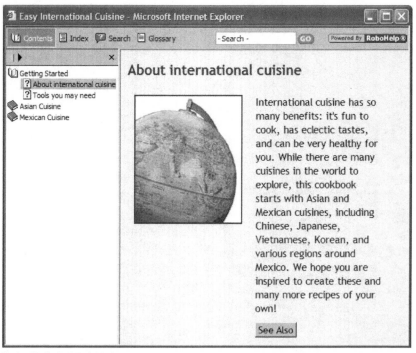

RoboHelp's WebHelp

Print targets

Target	Description
EPUB	A print format that is designed to be viewed online using a SmartPhone, tablet, or eReader device.
FrameMaker document	A print format that creates Adobe FrameMaker .book and .fm documents.
MOBI	A print format that is designed to be viewed on a Kindle.
PDF document	A print format developed by Adobe. The PDF format combines all of your topics and images into one file with a .pdf ('Portable Document Format') extension.
Word document	A print format that creates Microsoft .doc or .docx documents.
XHTML document	A print and online format that combines all of your topics into one file with a .xhtml file extension. This format is sometimes used to send documents to a printing company.
XPS document	A print format developed by Microsoft. XPS is similar to Adobe's PDF format, but it is based on XML. XPS combines all of your topics into one file with a .xps ('XML Paper Specification') extension.

'What is EPUB?'

EPUB is an online book format developed by the International Digital Publishing Forum (IDPF). It was designed and developed to format books for reading on electronic devices.

'What is MOBI?"

MOBI is an online book format that is owned by Amazon. It is used to create content for the Kindle. If you build an EPUB target, you can also build a MOBI version.

'What is XPS?'

XPS stands for 'XML Paper Specification.' It was created by Microsoft, but it has been released under a royalty-free copyright license. An XPS

Document package should appear the same on any computer. The two main differences between the PDF and XPS formats are that an XPS Document package is a .zip file (with a .xps extension instead of .zip), and XPS is based on XML.

Creating a target

You should create a different target for each version of your online help or print documents. For example, if you need to create WebHelp and print documentation for the 'Standard' and 'Professional' versions of your product, you should create four targets.

Shortcut	Tool Strip	Ribbon
Ctrl+T	📄 (Content Explorer)	File > New

To create a target:

1 Select **File** > **New**.
   —OR—
   Right-click the **Targets** folder and select **Add Target**.

   The Add File dialog box appears.

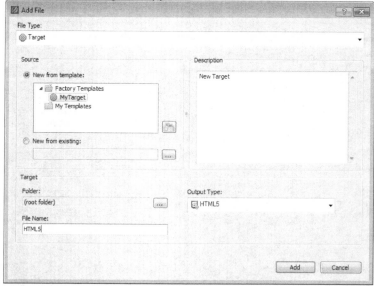

2 For **File Type**, select **Target**.

3 Select a **Source** template.

4 Type a **File Name**.
You don't have to type the .fltar extension. Flare will add it for you if you leave it out.

5 Select an **Output Type**.

6 Click **Add**.
The target appears in the Targets folder in the Project Organizer and opens in the Target Editor.

Specifying the primary target

The primary target is the target that you plan to create the most often. When you preview a topic, the topic will appear as it will appear in the primary target.

To specify the primary target:

□ Right-click a target and select **Make Primary**.

Setting up an online target

You can specify the skin, master page, TOC, condition tags, variables, and glossaries that are used in your online target.

To set up an online target:

1 Open the target.

2 On the **General** tab, select the following options:

□ **Output Type** — the help format that you are creating.

□ **Comment** — a short description of the target.

□ **Startup Topic** — the first topic that appears when the user opens your help system.

□ **Skin** — the skin file specifies the size, appearance, and features included in a target.

□ **Master TOC** — the TOC that will be used for the target.

- □ **Browse Sequence** – the browse sequence that will be used for the target.

- □ **Master Page Layout** – the page layout that will be used for all topics in a print target. Setting the master page layout will override page layouts that have been applied to specific topics.

- □ **Master Stylesheet** – the stylesheet that will be used for all topics. Setting the master stylesheet will override stylesheets that have been applied to specific topics.

- □ **Output File** – the name of the main entry (or 'start') file for your help system.

- □ **Output Folder** – where the generated help files will be created.

3 Select the **Conditional Text** tab.

4 Select whether you want to include or exclude each tag. See 'Including or excluding a tag when you build a target' on page 248.

5 Select the **Variables** tab.

6 If you need to change a variable's definition for the target, click inside its **Definition** cell and type a new value.

7 If you want to publish your online help to a file or web server:

- □ Select the **Publishing** tab.

- □ Select a destination.
  —OR—
  Click **New Destination** to create a publishing destination.

8 Select the **Glossary** tab and select the following options:

- □ **Glossary Term Conversion** method – how your glossary terms are converted in your topics.

- □ **Glossary** – the glossary (or glossaries) that are included in your target.

9 If you are using relationship tables and links, select the **Relationship Table** tab and select the relationship tables to use in your target.

10 Select the **Advanced** tab and select the options you would like to use. Commonly-set options include:

☐ **Insert Mark of the Web** – select to avoid Internet Explorer's 'active content' message when you open your WebHelp files locally.

⬦ The Mark of the Web option may prevent links to non-HTML files (such as PDFs) from working correctly.

☐ **Master Page** – select a master page to apply to your topics.

☐ **Generate Sitemap** – creates a sitemap to improve search engine optimization (SEO).

11 If you are building a large (8,000+ topic) DotNet Help, WebHelp, or HTML5 target, select the **Performance** tab and set the following options:

☐ **Index** – pre-merging the index file and using smaller index 'chunks' can make the index open faster for the user.

☐ **TOC** – using smaller TOC chunks can make the TOC open faster for the user.

☐ **Search Database** – you can exclude non-words from search (such as code examples), pre-merge the search or using smaller search chunks to make the search open faster for the user, and use larger n-grams to make a Japanese, Chinese, or Korean language search more accurate.

12 If you are using MadCap Pulse, select the **Community** tab, select the **Enable Pulse/Feedback Server** option, and type your server's URL.

13 If you are creating a WebHelp target, select the **Language** tab and select a language for the skin.

14 If you creating an HTML5 or WebHelp target, select the **Warnings** tab to turn on or off accessibility warnings. Accessibility warnings help you make your content more usable for users with disabilities.

15 Click **Save**.

Setting up a print target

You can create a print target to specify the condition tags, variables, and glossaries that are used in your print documentation.

To set up a print target:

1 Open the target.

2 On the **General** tab, select the following options:

- ☐ **Output Type** — the help format that you are creating.

- ☐ **Comment** — a short description of the target.

- ☐ **Master TOC** — the TOC that will be used for the target.

- ☐ **Master Page Layout** — the page layout that will be used for all topics in a print target. Setting the master page layout will override page layouts that have been applied to specific topics.

- ☐ **Master Stylesheet** — the stylesheet that will be used for all topics. Setting the master stylesheet will override stylesheets that have been applied to specific topics.

- ☐ **Output File** — the name of the generated document.

  🖎 *To create a Word 2007 or later document, include the .docx extension.*

- ☐ **Output Folder** — where the generated files will be created.

3 Select the **Conditional Text** tab.

4 Select whether you want to include or exclude each tag. See 'Including or excluding a tag when you build a target' on page 248.

5 Select the **Variables** tab.

6 If you need to change a variable's definition for the target, click inside its Definition cell and type a new value.

7 If you want to publish your print document to a file or web server:

    ☐ Select the **Publishing** tab.

    ☐ Select a destination.
    —OR—
    Click **New Destination** to create a publishing destination.

8 Select the **Glossary** tab and select a **Glossary** (or glossaries) to include in your documentation.

9 If you are using relationship tables and links, select the **Relationship Table** tab and select the relationship tables to use in your target.

10 Select the **Advanced** tab and select the options you would like to use. The most commonly-set options are:

    ☐ **Generate TOC, Index, or Glossary Proxy** — select each option to automatically include a TOC, index, and/or glossary in your document. **NEW!**

    ☐ **Stylesheet Medium** — if your stylesheet contains a medium (most people use the 'print' medium), you can use the medium's styles or the stylesheet's default styles.

    ☐ **Expanding Text Effects** — select how expanding text should appear in your print documents.

    ☐ **Text Popup Effects** — select how text popups should appear in your print document.

    ☐ **Generated TOC** — select whether your heading levels should match your TOC or the heading tags you used in your topics. Also, select whether you want to create headings for unlinked books in your TOC.

- Multi-Document Native XPS/PDF Output — if you are creating a PDF or XPS document, select this option to create multiple documents based on chapter breaks in the TOC. See 'Specifying Chapter Breaks' on page 155.

- Generate Multiple Documents for MS Word Output — if you are creating a Word document, select this option to create multiple documents based on chapter breaks in the TOC. See 'Specifying Chapter Breaks' on page 155.

- Redacted Text — if you are using the redacted style property, you can set how it will appear in your print target.

11 If you are creating a PDF target, select the **PDF Options** tab and select the following options:

- Image Compression — set the **Compression** option to **Automatic** to use Flare's lossless compression for non-JPG images or select **JPG** to convert all images to JPGs with some compression.

- Document Properties — type a title, author, subject, and any keywords you want to include and select whether you want to include crop and registration marks or convert RGB colors to CMYK.

- Convert Spot Colors to Black and White — specify whether you want to convert any colors (except images) to black and white. **NEW!**

- PDF Tagging — specify whether you want to include tags that are used by accessibility applications such as screen readers.

- Initial View — select the magnification level, whether the Bookmarks panel should appear, the page layout, and the text for the title bar.

- Security — specify whether you want to require a password or if you want to restrict the user from printing, editing, or copying text and graphics.

12 Select the **Warnings** tab and turn on any warnings, such as warnings about missing accessibility features, that you would would like to receive when you build your target. ▉▉▉▉

13 If you are creating an EPUB target, select the **EPUB Options** tab and select the following options:

☐ **Meta data** — type a title, author, publisher, and any other document properties you want to include.

☐ **Cover page** — if you want to add a cover page, select a cover page image.

☐ **Validate Epub 3 output** — specify whether you want to validate the EPUB document using the free EpubCheck application.

☐ **Generate MOBI output** — specify whether you want to create a MOBI document based on your EPUB document using Amazon's free KindleGen application.

☐ **Image conversion** — specify whether you want to convert SVG images or MathXML equations to PNG images.

14 Click **Save**.

Building a target

By default, your generated targets are stored in a folder named 'Output.' You can change the default folder, but most users use the default folder.

Shortcut	Tool Strip	Ribbon
F6	(Review toolbar)	Project > Build Primary

To build a target:

1 Select the **Project** ribbon, click the down arrow beside the **Build Primary** button, and select a target.
—OR—
Right-click a target and select **Build**.

2   If you made any changes to the target, Flare will prompt you to save your changes. Click **Yes**.
    The Build Progress dialog box appears.

3   When the build is complete, click **Yes** to view the generated target.

⏩ *You can select **Project** > **Clean Project** to delete everything in the Output folder.*

Building a target from the command line

Flare targets can be compiled from the command line. This feature can be used to build your targets from a batch file when you compile an application.

To build a target from the command line:

1   Open a command prompt.

2   Navigate to the directory where you installed Flare.
    The default directory for Flare 10 is
    program files (x86)\madcap software\madcap flare v10\flare.app.

3   Type madbuild -project <path><projectname> -target <targetname>.
    For example:
    ```
    madbuild -project c:\myFolder\myProject.flprj
    -target myWebHelp
    ```

To build all of your targets from the command line:

1   Open a command prompt.

2   Navigate to the directory where you installed Flare.
    The default directory for Flare 10 is
    program files (x86)\madcap software\madcap flare v10\flare.app.

3   Type **madbuild -project <path><projectfilename>**.
    For example:
    ```
    madbuild -project c:\myFolder\myProject.flprj
    ```

Saving the build log NEW!

After you build a target in Flare, you can save the build log. The build log contains a list of any messages and errors from the build, and it can be used to troubleshoot problems with your project. If you build from the command line, you can set Flare to automatically save the build log file.

To automatically save the build log file:

1 Select **File** > **Options**.

2 Select the **Build** tab.

3 Select **Save log on build**.

4 Click **OK**.

Batch generating targets

You can create a batch target to build and/or publish multiple targets. You can even schedule a batch target to run at a specific time every day, week, or month.

Shortcut	Tool Strip	Ribbon
Ctrl+T	(Content Explorer)	File > New

To create a batch generate target:

1 Select **File** > **New**.
  —OR—
  Right-click the **Targets** folder and select **Add Batch Target**.

The Add File dialog box appears.

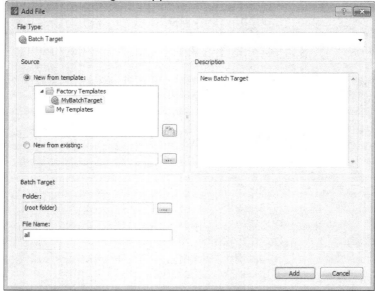

2 For **File Type**, select **Batch Target**.

3 Type a **File Name**.
   You don't have to type the .fltar extension. Flare will add it for
   you if you leave it out.

4 Click **Add**.
   The batch target appears in the Targets folder in the Project
   Organizer and opens in the Target Editor.

5 On the **Targets** tab, select the target(s) you want to build
   and/or publish.

6 Click **Save**.

To schedule a batch generate target:

1 Open a batch target.

2 Select the **Schedule** tab.

3 Click **New**.

The New Trigger dialog box appears.

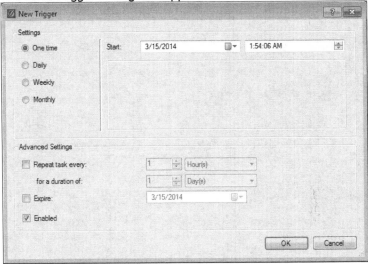

4 Select a frequency **Setting**.

5 Select a **Start** date and time.

6 If you selected a daily, weekly, or monthly frequency setting, select the recurrence details.

7 If the batch generate should repeat, select **Repeat task every** and specify how often and how long the repeating should occur.

8 If the repeating should expire, select **Expire** and specify an expiration date.

9 If you are ready to enable the batch generate, select **Enable**.

10 Click **OK**.

Viewing a target

Shortcut	Tool Strip	Ribbon
Shift+F6	(Review toolbar)	Project > View Primary

To view a target:

☐ Select the **Project** ribbon, click the down arrow beside the **View Primary** button, and select a target.
—OR—
Right-click a target and select **View**.

Publishing a target

You can publish any target to a file server or an FTP server. If you create multiple publishing destinations, you can publish to multiple destinations at the same time.

Shortcut	Tool Strip	Ribbon
Ctrl+T	▤ (Content Explorer)	File > New

To create a publishing destination:

1 Select **File** > **New**.
   —OR—
   Right-click the **Destinations** folder and select **Add Destination**. The Add File dialog box appears.

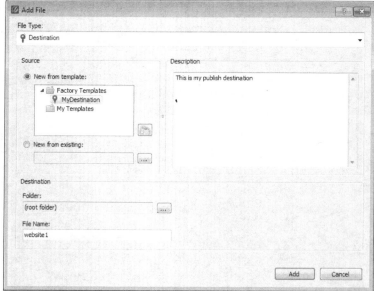

2 For **File Type**, select **Destination**.

3 Select a **Source** template.

4 Type a **File Name**.

5 Click **Add**.

The destination appears in the Destinations folder in the Project Organizer and opens in the Destination Editor.

6 Select a destination **Type**.

7 Type a **Comment**.

8 Click **Browse** to select a publishing directory.

9 If you are creating an FTP destination, click **Login Credentials** to provide your user name and password.

10 Select **Remove Stale Files** to remove deleted files from the destination when you republish.

11 Click **Save**.

To publish a target:

1 Open a target.

2 Select the **Publishing** tab.

3 Select one (or more) of the publishing destinations.

4 Select **Upload Only Changed Files** to only republished files that have changed.

5 Select **Remove Stale Files** to remove files from the server that have been removed from your project.

6 Click ⬚ Publish.

Flare copies the generated files to the publishing destination.

Context-sensitive help

Context-sensitive help (or 'CSH' if you like acronyms) is help that opens to a specific topic based on where you are in an application. For example, a 'Print Preview' dialog box would open a help topic about printing, and a 'Save' dialog box would open a topic about saving a file.

To create context-sensitive help, you need to associate your help topics to the windows and dialog boxes that are used in your application. This process is called 'mapping,' and it uses two files: header files and alias files.

Adding a header file

A header file is used to assign a number and an identifier to each dialog box and window in an application. Many programming applications create header files automatically, but you can also create header files using Flare. Header files have a .h or .hh extension, and they appear in the Advanced folder in the Project Organizer.

Header files use the following format:
```
#define MyID number
```

For example:
```
#define Save_dialog 1000
```

Shortcut	Tool Strip	Ribbon
Ctrl+T	▤ (Content Explorer)	File > New

To create a header file:

If your software team has created a header file, you can copy it to the Advanced folder in the Project folder. If you need to create a header file, follow these steps.

1 Select **File** > **New.**

—OR—

Right-click the **Advanced** folder and select **Add Header File.**
The Add File dialog box appears.

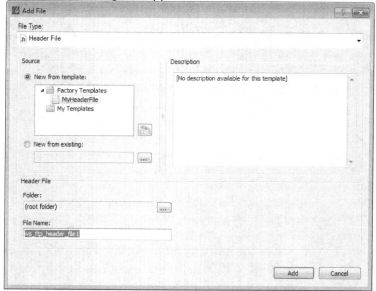

2 For **File Type,** select **Header File.**

3 Select a **Source** template.

4 Type a **File Name** for the header file.
You don't have to type the .h extension. Flare will add it for
you if you leave it out.

5 Click **Add.**
The header file appears in the Advanced folder in the Project
Organizer and opens in the Text Editor.

Creating an alias file

Alias files are used to match identifiers to a help topic. At first, an alias file might seem unnecessary: why not just put everything in the header file? The reason is that you need to share the header file with the development team. They need it to compile the application, and their programming application might automatically update the header file. By using an alias file, you can keep linking topics to identifiers while the developers are creating the application.

In Flare, alias files can also be used to assign a skin to a help topic when it is opened from the application. For example, you could normally open your help system in a large, 700x500 window with the navigation pane on the left. When you open it from a context-sensitive link, it could open in a smaller window without the navigation pane.

Alias files have a .flali extension. They appear in the Project Organizer in the Advanced folder.

Shortcut	Tool Strip	Ribbon
Ctrl+T	(Content Explorer)	File > New

To create an alias file:

1 Select **File** > **New**.
  —OR—
  Right-click the **Advanced** folder and select **Add Alias File**.
  The Add File dialog box appears.

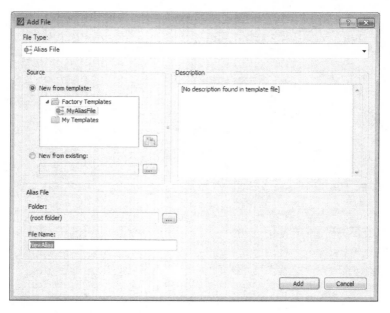

2 For **File Type**, select **Alias File**.

3 Select a **Source** template.

4 Type a **File Name** for the alias file.
You don't have to type the .flali extension. Flare will add it for you if you leave it out.

5 Click **Add**.
The alias file appears in the Advanced folder in the Project Organizer and opens in the Alias Editor.

To assign an identifier to a topic:

1 Open the alias file.
Alias files are stored in the Advanced folder in the Project Organizer.

2 On the right side of the Alias Editor, select an identifier.

3 On the left side of the Alias Editor, select a topic to link to the identifier.

4 Double-click the topic.
–OR–
Click .
The topic's filename appears in the **Topic** column.

5 Continue assigning topics to identifiers.

6 Save your alias file.
You can open your alias file and add new identifiers at any time.

Testing context-sensitive help

After you assign identifiers to your topics, you can test your context-sensitive help links.

To test your context-sensitive help:

1 Build your target.

2 Right-click your target and select **Test CSH API Calls**.
The Context-sensitive Help API Tester dialog box appears.

3 Next to each identifier, click .
The correct help topic should appear.

Sample questions for this section

1   Which output types were created by MadCap software? (select all
    that apply)
    A) DotNet Help
    B) HTML Help
    C) WebHelp
    D) XPS

2   How can you set up your WebHelp to not display the 'Active
    Content' message?
    A) Select **File** > **Options** and select **Disable Active Content**.
    B) Select **Disable Active Content** in your target.
    C) Select **Insert Mark of the Web** in your target.
    D) It should not appear for WebHelp. It only appears in HTML Help.

3   What is a primary target?
    A) The main or 'master' target in merged projects.
    B) The only target you can create from a project.
    C) A project you plan to link to another project.
    D) The target you expect to build the most often.

4   How many targets can you set up in a project?
    A) One
    B) One for each type (i.e., one HTML Help, one WebHelp, etc.)
    C) One for online and one for print.
    D) As many as you want.

5   What happens when you select **Project** > **Clean Project**?
    A) Flare fixes any incorrect XHTML code in your topics.
    B) Flare finds any files in the Content folder that are not being
    used.
    C) Flare deletes everything in the Output folder.
    D) Flare fixes any broken links.

6 What happens when you publish a target?

A) Flare creates the output files.

B) Flare copies the output files to a network or a website.

C) Flare prints the output files.

D) Flare creates a postscript file that you can send to a printer.

7 What is the 'startup' topic?

A) The topic that opens when you open the project in Flare.

B) The first topic that users see when they open the online target.

C) The file users double-click to open the target.

D) The file you double-click to open your project in Flare.

Project management

This section covers:

- ☐ Topic templates
- ☐ Contribution templates
- ☐ Spell check
- ☐ Find and replace **NEW!**
- ☐ File tags
- ☐ Reports
- ☐ Track changes
- ☐ Annotations
- ☐ Topics reviews **NEW!**
- ☐ Pulse
- ☐ Source control
- ☐ SharePoint integration
- ☐ Project archiving **NEW!**

Templates

Everything you create in Flare, including topics, stylesheets, master pages, and page layouts, is based on a template. Templates are just a 'starting point' when you create a file. The new topic is not linked to the template, so any changes you make to the template will not be made to the topics that were created based on the template.

Creating a topic template

If your topics always have a similar structure, such as a heading, paragraph, table, and list, you can create a template to start your topics with these blocks of content.

Shortcut	Tool Strip	Ribbon
none	File > Save as Template	File > Save > Save as Template

To create a topic template:

1 Open the topic that you want to become a template.

2 Add any content you want to include in the template.

3 Format the content.

4 Select **File** > **Save** > **Save as Template**.
The Save as Template dialog box appears.

5 Type a **Template Name**.

6 Click **OK**.
Your template will be available in the My Templates folder. Topic templates use the same extension as topics: .htm.

TIP *By default, templates are stored in the My Documents\My Templates\Content folder on your PC. If you work on a team, you can move your templates to a file server. When you create a new topic, select 'New from existing' and click ⬜ to select the template on the file server.*

Creating a Contribution template

If other members of your team are using Contributor to create topics, you can create a Contribution template. A Contribution template can include pre-formatted text, images, and tables to help them create topics using the correct styles.

Shortcut	Tool Strip	Ribbon
none	Tools > Contributions > Create Contribution Template	File > Save > Save as Contribution Template

To create a Contribution template:

1 Open the topic that you want to become a template.

2 Add any content to the topic that you want to include.

3 If you want to prevent a user from modifying part of the topic:

☐ Highlight the content.

☐ Select **Review** > **Lock**.

4 Select **File** > **Save** > **Save as Contribution Template**.
The Save Topic as Contribution Template wizard appears.

5 Type a **Template Name**.

6 Select a template location.
By default, Contribution templates are stored in the Documents\My Templates\Content folder on your PC.

7 Click **Next**.

8 Select any content files the template uses, such as images, page layouts, master pages, snippets, or stylesheets.

9 Click **Next**.

10 Select any condition tag sets or variable sets the template uses.

11 Click **Finish**.

The Contribution template is saved. Contribution templates use the .mccot extension.

12 Click **Yes** if you want to email the Contribution template to a contributor.

▣▷ *If you work on a team, you can move your Contribution templates to a file server. When contributors create a new topic, they can select 'New from existing' and click* ▭ *to select the Contribution template on the file server.*

Spell check

You can spell check a topic, the entire project, or while you are editing a topic in the XML Editor. You can also create a list of terms to ignore when spell checking and add language dictionaries.

Spell checking a topic or project

Shortcut	Tool Strip	Ribbon
F7	Tools > Spell Check Window	Tools > Spell Check Window

To spell check a topic:

1 Open a topic.

2 Select **Tools** > **Spell Check Window**.
   —OR—
   Press **F7**.
   The Spell Check window appears.

3 For **Start Spell Check**, select the topics you want to spell check.

4 For each potential misspelled word, click **Skip**, **Ignore**, **Add to Dictionary**, or **Ignore in All Files** or select a **Suggestion**.

To spell check a project:

1 Open any topic.

2 Select **Tools** > **Spell Check Window**.
   —OR—
   Press **F7**.
   The Spell Check window appears.

3 For **Start Spell Check**, select the topics you want to spell check

4 For each potential misspelled word, click **Skip, Ignore, Add to Dictionary,** or **Ignore in All Files** or select a **Suggestion.**

To enable or disable spell check while typing:

☐ Select **Tools > Spell Check While Typing.**

Ignoring words when spell checking

You can create a list of terms that you want to ignore when spell checking. For example, you might ignore acronyms, words with numbers, or technical and jargon terms.

Shortcut	Tool Strip	Ribbon
Alt+T, I	Tools > Ignored Words	Tools > Ignored Words

To ignore words when spell checking:

1 Select **Tools > Ignored Words.**
The Ignored Words dialog box appears.

2 Type the words you want to ignore.

3 Click **OK.**

Adding spell check dictionaries

Flare includes dictionaries for numerous languages and country-specific language variants. You can download and install open-source dictionaries for other languages.

Many dictionaries are available at:
extensions.services.openoffice.org/dictionary

Shortcut	Tool Strip	Ribbon
Alt+F, T	Tools > Options	File > Options

To add a spell checking dictionary:

1 Select **File** > **Options**.
The Options dialog box appears.

2 Select the **Dictionaries** tab.
Installed dictionaries are indicated with a green dot in the Spell column.

3 Click **Import Dictionaries**.
The Select dictionary files dialog box appears.

4 Select a dictionary.
Dictionary files have a .oxt extension.

5 Click **Open**.

Find and replace

You can find or find and replace content within a topic, all of the topics in a folder, or all of the topics in a project. Flare includes standard options such as case sensitivity and searching in the source code, it also provides advanced options such as using wildcards and regular expressions.

Finding content in a topic NEW!

Shortcut	Tool Strip	Ribbon
Ctrl+F	Edit > Find and Replace	Home > Quick Find

To find content in a topic:

1 Select **Home** > **Quick Find**.
  —OR—
  Press **Ctrl+F**.
  The Quick Find widget appears.

2 In the text box, type the text you want to find.

3 If you want to only match whole words, click and select **Whole word**.

4 If you want to make the find case sensitive, click and select **Match case**.

5 If you want to use wildcard or regular expressions, click and select **Wildcards** or **Regular expressions**.

6 Click **Find Previous** or **Find Next**.

Finding and replacing in a topic 🔳NEW🔳

Shortcut	Tool Strip	Ribbon
Ctrl+H	Edit > Find and Replace	Home > Quick Replace

To find and replace content in a topic:

1 In the **Find** text box, type the text you want to find.

2 In the **Replace** text box, type the text you want to add.

3 If you want to only match whole words, click 🔲 and select **Whole word.**

4 If you want to make the find case sensitive, click 🔲 and select **Match case.**

5 If you want to use wildcard or regular expressions, click 🔲 and select **Wildcards** or **Regular expressions.**

6 Click **Replace Next** or **Replace All.**

Finding and replacing in multiple topics

Shortcut	Tool Strip	Ribbon
Ctrl+Shift+F	Edit > Find and Replace	Home > Find and Replace in Files

To find and replace content in multiple topics:

1 Select **Home** > **Find and Replace in Files.**
   —OR—
   Press **Ctrl+Shift+F.**
   The File and Replace in Files dialog box appears.

2 In the **Find** text box, type the text you want to find.

3 Select a **Find in** option.

4 Select the type of file(s) you want to search.

5 Select **Match case** if you want to make the find case sensitive.

6 Select **Whole word** if you want to only match whole words and not parts of words.

7 Select **Find in source code** if you want to also find matches in the code.

8 Select **Use wildcards** or **Use regular expressions** to create an advanced find expression.

9 Select results window 1 or 2.

10 Click **Find All**.
The find results appear in the results window.

Using wildcards and regular expressions

You can use wildcards and regular expressions to create advanced find expressions. Wildcards are useful for partial searches, such as finding all phone numbers with a specified area code. Regular expressions are much more advanced and can be used to find all h1s or spans or a word if it is near another word.

Wildcard examples

Find expression	Result
404-*	Finds "404-555-5555," "404-555-0000", etc.
.*.com	Finds "mysite.com," "yoursite.com," etc.
locali?e	Finds "localize" and "localise"
locali*	Finds" localize, "localization," "localise," and "localisation"

For more information about wildcards, see:
en.wikipedia.org/wiki/Wildcard_character

Regular expression examples

Find expression	Result
<h1\b[^>]*>(.*?)</h1>	Finds all h1s
\bquick\W+(?:\w+\W+){1,5}?fox\b	Finds the word "quick" only if it is within five words of the word "fox"

Flare supports .NET Framework regular expressions. For more information, see msdn.microsoft.com/en-us/library/hs600312.aspx

File tags and reports

You can create file tags to specify authors, status levels, or any other type of information for files in your project. For example, you could create a 'reviewer' tag to track who the subject-matter expert reviewer should be for each topic. File tags can be assigned to any type of file in your project.

Creating a file tag set

Flare provides templates to create author and status file tags, and you can modify them as needed. Or, you can create your own file tag set.

Shortcut	Tool Strip	Ribbon
Ctrl+T	(Content Explorer toolbar)	File > New

To create a file tag set:

1 Select **File** > **New**.

The Add File dialog box appears.

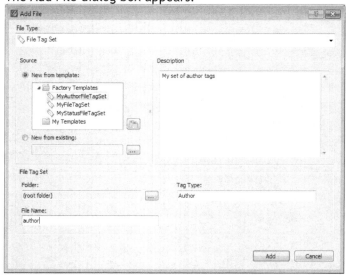

2 For **File Type**, select **File Tag Set**.

3 Select a **Source** template.

4 Type a **File Name**.

5 Click **Add**.
The file tag set file appears in the Advanced folder in the Project Organizer and opens in the File Tag Set Editor.

To add a tag to a file tag set:

1 Open a file tag set.

2 Click 📰.
The new tag appears.

3 Type a name for the tag.

To apply a tag:

1 Right-click a file and select **Properties**.
The Properties dialog box appears.

2 Select the **File Tag** tab.

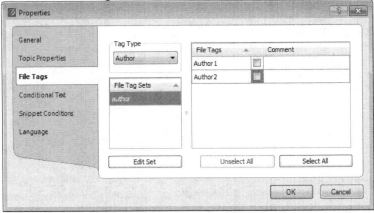

3 Select a **Tag Type**.

4 Select a **File Tag**.

5 Click **OK**.

Creating a report

You can create reports based on your file tags, or you can create report that include any of the following information:

Bookmarks

☐ Broken bookmarks

☐ Unused bookmarks

☐ Used bookmarks

Concepts

☐ Concept links

☐ Files with concepts

☐ Topics with concept links

☐ Topics with concept links missing a concept

☐ Used concepts

☐ Used search filters

Condition tags

☐ Applied conditions

☐ Files with condition tags

☐ Topics with snippet conditions

☐ Undefined condition tags

☐ Unused condition tags

☐ Used condition tags

Content files

☐ Empty content folders

☐ Files with changes (includes annotations)

☐ Files with concepts

☐ Files with condition tags

☐ Files with equations

☐ Files with file tags

☐ Files with glossary term links

☐ Files with images

☐ Files with keywords

☐ Files with language tags

☐ Files with multimedia

☐ Files with named destinations

☐ Files with QR codes

☐ Files with snippets

☐ Files with variables

☐ Unused content files

Context-sensitive help

☐ Assigned CSH IDs

☐ Duplicate Map IDs

☐ Topics Linked By Map ID

☐ Topics Not Linked By Map ID

☐ Unused CSH IDs

File tags

☐ Files with file tags

☐ Undefined file tags

☐ Unused file tags

☐ Used file tags

Glossary Term Links

☐ Files with glossary term links

☐ Undefined glossary term links

☐ Used glossary term links

Images

- Files with images
- Unused images
- Used images

Index

- Files with keywords
- Index keyword links
- Index keyword suggestions
- Topics not in index
- Topics with index keyword links
- Topics with keyword links missing a keyword
- Used index keywords

Language tags

- Files with language tags
- Used language tags

Links

- Absolute links
- Broken bookmarks
- Broken links
- Broken snippet links
- Concept links
- Cross reference suggestions
- External links
- Index keyword links
- Named destinations
- Topics linked by map ID
- Topics not linked
- Topics not linked by map ID
- Topics with concept links

- Topics with concept links missing a concept
- Topics with index keyword links
- Topics with keyword links missing a keyword
- Undefined glossary term links
- Unused bookmarks
- Used bookmarks
- Used glossary term links

Multimedia

- Files with multimedia
- Unused multimedia
- Used multimedia

Project

- Database errors
- Statistics

Snippets

- Broken snippet links
- Files with snippets
- Snippet suggestions
- Topics with snippet conditions
- Unused snippets
- Used snippets

Styles

- Duplicate styles
- New style suggestions
- Replace local style suggestions
- Undefined styles
- Unused styles

☐ Used stylesheets

TOC

☐ Duplicate TOC items

☐ TOC - primary target

☐ Topics not in any TOC

Topics

☐ Accessibility suggestions

☐ Broken bookmarks

☐ Broken links

☐ Cross reference suggestions

☐ Markup suggestions

☐ Non-XML topics

☐ Topics linked by map ID

☐ Topics not in any TOC

☐ Topics not in index

☐ Topics not linked

☐ Topics not linked by map ID

☐ Topics with concept links

☐ Topics with concept links missing a concept

☐ Topics with index keyword links

☐ Topics with keyword links missing a keyword

☐ Topics with snippet conditions

☐ Writing suggestions

Variables

☐ Files with variables

☐ Undefined variables

☐ Unused variables

☐ Used variables

☐ Variable suggestions

To create a report file:

1 Select **File** > **New.**

—OR—

Right-click the **Reports** folder and select **Add Report File.**

The Add File dialog box appears.

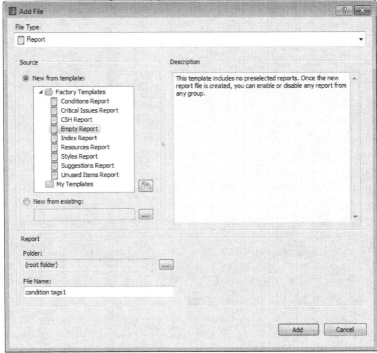

2   For **File Type**, select **Report File**.

3   Select a **Source** template.

4   Type a **File Name**.

5   Click **Add**.
    The report appears in the Reports folder in the Project
    Organizer and opens in the Report Editor.

To generate, save, or print a report:

1   Open a report.

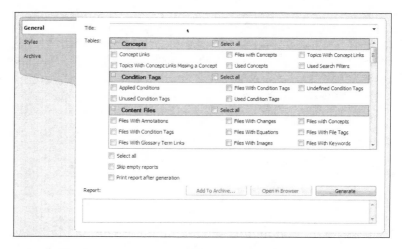

2 On the **General** tab, type a **Title** for the report.

3 Select the **Tables** to include in the report.

4 If you want to change the report's formatting, click the **Styles** tab and changes the style properties.

5 On the **General** tab, click **Generate**.

6 To print or save the report, click **Open in Browser**.

Track changes, annotations, and reviews

Tracking changes

You can enable track changes to capture changes made to a topic, snippet, or master page. If you enable track changes, the changes are stored in the code. If you reject the change, you can restore the original version.

Track changes are very useful during topic reviews, since the reviewers can see exactly how the content has changed.

Shortcut	Tool Strip	Ribbon
Ctrl+Shift+E	(Review toolbar)	Review > Track Changes

To track changes:

1 Open a topic.

2 Select **Review** > **Track Changes**.

3 Change the topic as needed.

To hide or show tracked changes:

1 Open a topic.

2 Select **Review** > **Show Changes**.

To accept or reject a tracked change:

1 Open a topic.

2 Select **Review** > **Show Changes**.

3 To select a specific change, click the change and select **Review** > **Accept Change**.
  To accept all changes, select **Review** > **Accept All Changes**.

To customize how changes display:

1 Select **Review** > **Review Options**.
  The Options dialog box appears.

2 Type your **User Name**.

3 Type your **Initials**.

4 Select a **Tracked Changes Display** option.

5 Select a **User Colors** option.

Annotations

You can add annotations to your topics to keep notes or to track your development progress. If you send topics for review, reviewers can use Contributor to add annotations. Annotations are not included when you build a target.

Adding an annotation

You can add an annotation anywhere in a topic, and you can add as many annotations as you need.

Shortcut	Tool Strip	Ribbon
Alt+R, W	▤ (Review toolbar)	Review > Insert Annotation

To add an annotation:

1 Open a topic.

2 Select the content that you would like to annotate.

3 Select **Review** > **Insert Annotation**.
   The Edit Annotation Pane appears.

4 If this is your first annotation, type your initials.

5 Type your annotation.

To show or hide annotations:

1 Open a topic.

2 Select **Review** > **Show Changes**.

Locking content

You can lock content so that it cannot be edited. For example, you might lock a paragraph so that a reviewer using Contributor can see it but not change it.

To lock content so that it cannot be edited:

1 Open a topic.

2 Position your cursor inside the content you want to lock.

3 Select **Review** > **Lock**.
   The paragraphs are locked and cannot be edited.

Sending topics for review NEW!

You can create a review package to send multiple topics and/or snippets for review. If your topics contain snippets, the snippets will be automatically included in the review package.

If you send your topics using the TOC, Flare will include the TOC and all of the topics that are linked to by the selected book and its sub-books and pages. Reviewers can use Contributor to revise your topics, add annotations, and return the reviewed topics.

Shortcut	Tool Strip	Ribbon
Alt+R, S	▦ (Review toolbar)	Review > Send for Review

To send topics for review:

1 Select **Review** > **Send for Review**.
The Send Topic for Review wizard appears.

2 Type a **Review Package Name**.

3 If you have defined multiple definitions for your variables and selected different definitions for your targets, select a target to specify the variable definitions that will appear in your review topics. **NEW!**

4 If you use condition tags in the selected topics, click ▦ to include or exclude content in your review topics based on their condition tags. **NEW!**

5 Click ▦.
The Open File dialog box appears.

6 Select the topics you want to send for review and click **Open**.

◇ *If a selected topic contains a snippet, the snippet will also be added to the review package.* **NEW!**

7 Click **Next**.

8 Type a subject and message for the email.

9 Click **Add Email Recipient** to select a recipient.

10 Click **Send**.
Your email application opens.

11 Send the email.

To send topics for review using the TOC:

1 Open a TOC.

2 Right-click a book and select **Send for Review**.
The Send Topic for Review wizard appears.

3 Type a **Review Package Name**.

4 Click **Next**.

5 Type a subject and message for the email.

6 Click **Add Email Recipient** to select a recipient.

7 Click **Send**.
Your email application opens.

8 Send the email.

To view a list of topics that have been sent for review:

1 Select **Review** > **Topic Reviews**.

2 In the text box at the top of the window, select **Sent Topics**.

Accepting review edits

If you allow reviewers to edit a topic using Contribute, you can accept the reviewed topic. When you accept the reviewed topic, the original topic is replaced by the reviewed topic.

Shortcut	Tool Strip	Ribbon
Alt+R, T	🔍 (Review toolbar)	Review > Topic Reviews

To accept reviewed topics:

1 Select **Review** > **Topic Reviews**.

2 In the text box at the top of the window, select **Inbox**.

3 Select a topic.

4 Click 🗐 and click **OK**.

Setting review display options

You can specify how track changes and annotations appear in the XML Editor.

To set the review display options:

1 Select **File** > **Flare Options**.

2 Select the **Review** tab.

3 Type your **User Name**.

4 Type your **Initials**.

5 Select a **Tracked Changes Display** option.

6 Select a **User Colors** option.

Pulse

Like Feedback (which it replaces), you can use MadCap Pulse to add user commenting to WebHelp and HTML5 targets. However, Pulse is a more robust, social collaboration platform. In addition to adding comments, users can like topics, ask and answer questions, and post files, articles, and images.

Setting up Pulse

You can install Pulse on the same server as your WebHelp or HTML5 content (the recommended approach), or you can install Pulse on a separate server. The Pulse server will need:

☐ Microsoft Windows Server 2008 or 2008 R2

☐ Microsoft .NET Framework 3.5.1 and 4.0

☐ Microsoft SQL Server 2008 Standard or 2008 R2

☐ Microsoft Internet Information Server (IIS) 7

☐ Microsoft ASP.NET 4.0

Pulse user levels

Pulse provides four user levels: unregistered ("general public"), basic ("customer"), advanced ("employee"), and administrator. The following table summarizes the tasks that each type of user can perform:

Task	Unregistered	Basic	Advanced	Admin
Read comments	✓	✓	✓	✓
Search comments	✓	✓	✓	✓
See ratings and interactions	✓	✓	✓	✓
Rate topics		✓	✓	✓
Create user profiles		✓	✓	✓

Task	Unregistered	Basic	Advanced	Admin
Post status updates		✓	✓	✓
Comment on, like, and follow posts		✓	✓	✓
Upload files		✓	✓	✓
Subscribe to topics		✓	✓	✓
Delete and edit their posts		✓	✓	✓
Assign tasks			✓	✓
Message users			✓	✓
Mark favorites			✓	✓
Vote on answers			✓	✓
Filter and view files			✓	✓
Access groups			✓	✓
Delete posts or files				✓
Modify server settings				✓
View reports				✓

Enabling Pulse in a skin

You can set up a skin to include the Pulse community tab and display user comments at the bottom of your topics.

To enable Pulse in a skin:

1 Open a skin.
The Skin Editor appears.

2 Select the **General** tab.

3 Select the **Community** option.

4 Select the **Community** tab.

5 Select the **Display topic comments at the end of each topic** option.

6 Select the **Display Community Search Results** option.
The total number of search results will display in parenthesis beside the Community Results heading in the search results.

Enabling Pulse in a target

You can add Pulse to WebHelp, WebHelp Plus, or HTML5 targets.

To enable Pulse for a target:

1 Open a target.

2 Select the **Community** tab.

3 Select **Enable Pulse/Feedback Server**.

4 Type your Pulse server's **URL**.

5 Click **Login**.
The Login dialog box appears.

6 Type your **User name**.

7 Type your **Password**.

8 Click **OK**.

9 In the **Communities** field, select your Pulse community.

10 Save the target.

Creating a Pulse profile

Pulse users can create a profile themselves to interact with topics and other users, or they can be invited to join the Pulse community by the administrator.

To create a Pulse profile:

1 Open a WebHelp or HTML5 output that uses Pulse.

2 Select the **Community** tab or open a topic.

3 Click **Register**.

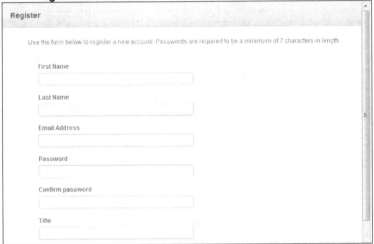

4 Type your **First Name** and **Last Name**.

5 Type your **Email Address**.

6 Type and confirm your **Password**.

7 Click **Register**.
You will receive a registration email.

8 Open your email and complete the registration.

Editing your Pulse profile

You can edit your Pulse avatar, contact information, and notification options, such as whether you receive an email when other users comment on your posts.

To edit your profile:

1 Open a WebHelp or HTML5 output that uses Pulse.

2 Select the **Community** tab.

3 Click **Edit My Profile**.
The Settings window appears.

4 Select the **Personal** tab to change your information or select the **Notifications** tab to change your notification options.

Viewing notifications

You can use the Notifications window to view summary of your posts, tasks, questions, and groups, or any activities for people you are following.

To view notifications:

1 Open a WebHelp or HTML5 output that uses Pulse.

2 Select the **Community** tab.

3 Click **Notifications**.
The Notifications window appears.

Viewing a report

MadCap Pulse provides the following reports:

- Browser statistics
- Context-sensitive help calls
- Most active groups
- Operating system statistics
- Overall activity
- Search phrases

- Most commented activities
- Most commented file shares
- Most commented image shares
- Most liked link shares
- Most liked people
- Search phrases with no results
- Storage usage
- Topics
- User activity
- User count

To view a report:

1 Open your Pulse Admin site in a browser.

2 Click **Administration**.

3 Select **Reports**.
A list of reports appears.

4 Click a report.

5 If you have multiple Pulse communities, you can filter the reports by community.

Source control

You can add (or 'bind') your project to any source control application that supports the Microsoft Source Code Control API (SCC API), including:

- ClearCase

- CVS

- Git

- Perforce

- Subversion (SVN)

- Team Foundation Server (TFS)

- Visual SourceSafe (VSS)

A source control application can prevent team members from overwriting each other's changes, save past versions of files, and identify changes made to files (and who made them).

Binding a project to source control

Flare provides built-in support for Microsoft's Visual SourceSafe (VSS) and Team Foundation Server (TFS) Apache's Subversion, and Perforce. With these applications, you can bind your project and check in/check out files within Flare. For other source control applications, you will need a plug-in to integrate the application with Flare. Or, you can check out the files in your source control application, use Flare to make changes, then check in the files outside of Flare.

Shortcut	Tool Strip	Ribbon
Alt+P, R	(Project toolbar)	Project > Project Properties

To bind a project to a source control application:

1 Select **Project** > **Project Properties**.
The Project Properties dialog box appears.

2 Select the **Source Control** tab.

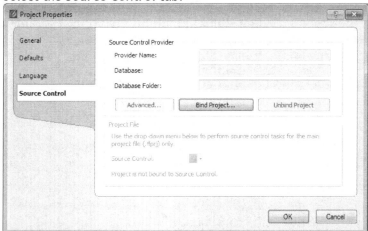

3 Click **Bind Project**.
The Bind Project dialog box appears.

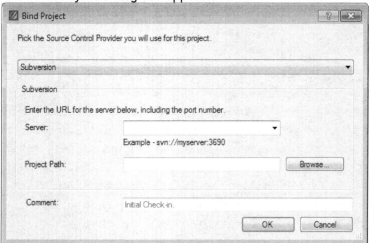

4 Select a **Source Control Provider** and provide the required information.

5 Click **OK**.

Adding a file to source control

When you add a file to your project, you can also add it to your source control application. A ✦ plus sign icon will appear beside new files that have not been added to source control.

Shortcut	Tool Strip	Ribbon
Alt+S, A	(Standard toolbar)	Source Control > Add

To add a file to source control:

1 Select a file or folder that is not in source control.

2 Select **Source Control** > **Add**.
   —OR—
   Right-click the file or folder and select **Source Control** > **Add**. The Check In dialog box appears.

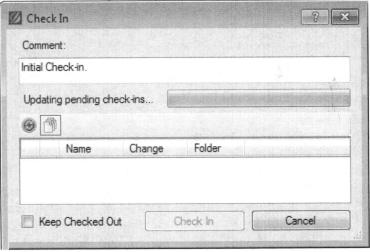

3 Type a **Comment**.

4 If you want to keep editing the file, select **Keep Checked Out**.

5 Click **Check In**.

Getting the latest version of a file

Before you make changes to a file, you should make sure you have the latest version from source control. A ⏱ clock icon will appear in the Content Explorer beside any local file that is older than the source control version.

Shortcut	Tool Strip	Ribbon
Alt+S, G, L	⬚ (Standard toolbar)	Source Control > Get Latest Version

To get the latest version of a file or folder:

1 Select a file or folder. If you want to get the latest version of all files in the Content Explorer, select the **Content** folder.

2 Select **Source Control** > **Get Latest Version**.
   —OR—
   Right-click the file and select **Source Control** > **Get Latest Version**.

3 If the local version matches the source control version, click **OK**. If the files are different, click **Merge All** or click **Resolve** to review the differences.

Checking out a file

You should check out a file before you modify it. When you check out a file, other users see a 🔒 icon beside it in the Content Explorer.

If you do not check out a file, other users may modify it while you are making changes. See 'Merging changes' on page 320 for information about resolving your changes.

Shortcut	Tool Strip	Ribbon
Alt+S, C, O	⬚ (Standard toolbar)	Source Control > Check Out

To check out a file:

1 Select a file or folder.

2 Select **Source Control** > **Check Out**.
   −OR−
   Right-click the file and select **Source Control** > **Check Out**.
   The Check Out dialog box appears.

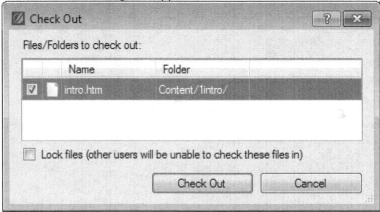

3 If you want to lock the files to prevent other users from
   checking out the file, select **Lock Files**.

4 Click **Check Out**.
   A ✓ checkmark icon appears beside the checked out files.

Checking in a file

After you have made changes to a file, you can check it in to source
control so that other users can work with it.

Shortcut	Tool Strip	Ribbon
Alt+S, C, I	🔲 (Standard toolbar)	Source Control > Check In

To check in a file:

1 Select a file or folder.

2 Select **Source Control** > **Check In**.

—OR—

Right-click the file and select **Source Control** > **Check In**.
The Check In dialog box appears.

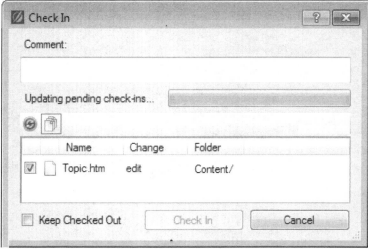

3   Type a check in **Comment**.

4   If you selected a folder, select **Recursive** if you want to add all of the files inside the folder.

5   Select **Keep Checked Out** if you want to check in the current version and keep editing the file.

6   Click **OK**.
A 🔒 lock appears beside the filename in the Content Explorer.

Viewing a list of checked out files

You can view a list of files that are checked out by you or other users.

Shortcut	Tool Strip	Ribbon
Alt+S, P	(Standard toolbar)	Source Control > Pending Check-Ins

To view a list of files that are checked out:

1   Select **Source Control** > **Pending Check-Ins**.
The Pending Check-Ins pane opens.

2 Scroll to the right to view the Status and User columns.

3 To sort the list, click a column heading.

Viewing differences between versions

You can compare any two versions of a file to review how a file has changed.

Shortcut	Tool Strip	Ribbon
Alt+S, S	(Standard toolbar)	Source Control > Show Differences

To view differences between versions:

1 Select a file.

2 Select **Source Control** > **Show Differences**.
The History dialog box appears.

3 Select two versions of the file.

4 Click **Show Differences**.

Rolling back to a previous version

You can roll back to a previous checked in version of a file.

Shortcut	Tool Strip	Ribbon
Alt+S, V	(Standard toolbar)	Source Control > View History

To roll back to a previous version:

1 Select a file or folder.

2 Select **Source Control** > **View History**.
—OR—
Right-click and select **Source Control** > **View History**.

The History dialog appears.

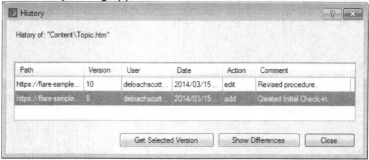

3   Select a version of the file.

4   Click **Get Selected Version**.
    The selected version will be copied to the project.

5   Click **Close**.

Merging changes

If two users have modified a file at the same time, you can merge the changes and try to preserve both user's modifications.

Shortcut	Tool Strip	Ribbon
Alt+S, C, I	(Standard toolbar)	Source Control > Check In

To merge changes:

1   Check in or get the latest version of a file.
    If your version is different from the version in source control, the Resolve Conflicts dialog box appears.

2   Click **Auto Merge All**.
    If the differences do not conflict, the versions are merged. If the differences conflict, complete the following steps.

3   Click **OK**.

4   Click **Resolve**.

5   Select a resolution option:

- □ **Merge changes in merge tool** – Opens a merging interface, which lets you see exactly what changes were made and choose which to keep.

- □ **Undo my local changes** – Automatically removes your changes and keeps changes from other authors.

- □ **Discard server changes** – Automatically removes changes from other authors and keeps your changes.

6 If you selected **Merge changes in merge tool**, you can:

- □ **Right-click** to open a context menu that can be used to keep or ignore a change to the server or local version.

- □ **Left-click** to keep the change to the server or local version.

- □ **Type** content to edit the content and merge the versions yourself.

7 Click **OK** when all of the conflicts are resolved.

SharePoint integration

You can import SharePoint files into your Flare project. For example, you can reuse PDFs, logos, or other documents that are stored in a company-wide SharePoint directory.

Connecting to a SharePoint server

If you connect your project to a SharePoint server, you can include files from SharePoint in your project.

Shortcut	Tool Strip and Ribbon
Alt+P, H	View > SharePoint Explorer

To connect to a SharePoint server:

1 Select **View** > **SharePoint Explorer**.
The SharePoint Explorer pane appears.

2 Click ▦.
The Connect to SharePoint Server dialog box appears.

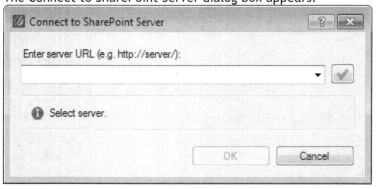

3 Type the path to the SharePoint server.

4 Click ☑ to validate the server's URL.

5 Click **OK**.
The SharePoint Explorer pane appears.

Copying and mapping SharePoint files

After you connect to a SharePoint server, you can add files from SharePoint to your project. If you map the files, you can synchronize any changes that are made to your local copy of the file or the version in SharePoint.

To copy and map SharePoint files:

1   Select **View** > **SharePoint Explorer**.
    The SharePoint Explorer pane appears.

2   Right-click a file and select **Copy to Project**.

3   Click **OK**.
    The Copy to Project dialog box appears.

4   Select **Keep file synchronized (create mapping)**.

5   Click **OK**.
    An orange icon appears beside the file in the Content Explorer.

Synchronizing SharePoint files

When you synchronize a file, Flare compares your local version of the file to the version in SharePoint. If they are different, you can update either version.

Shortcut	Tool Strip	Ribbon
Alt+P, Y	Tools > Synchronize Mapped Files	Project > Synchronize Files

To synchronize SharePoint files:

1   Select **Project** > **Synchronize Files**.
    The Synchronize Files dialog box appears.

2   Select one of the following options:

Option	Description
Synchronize Files	Compares the version of the files in your project to the version in SharePoint and updates the

Option	Description
	version that is out of date.
Import Files	Copies out-of-sync SharePoint files into your project, even if the files in your project have been modified more recently that the versions in SharePoint.
Export Files	Copies out-of-sync files in your project to SharePoint, even if the files in SharePoint have been modified more recently that the versions in your project.
Custom	Allows you to manually select which files you want to import or export.

3 Click **Synchronize**.

4 Click **OK**.

Checking out a file from SharePoint

If you check out a file, other users are not allowed to make changes to the file until you check it in again.

Shortcut	Tool Strip and Ribbon
Alt+F, H, O	File > SharePoint > Check Out

To check out a file:

1 Select the file(s) you want to check out.

2 Select **File > SharePoint > Check Out**.
  —OR—
  Right-click the file(s) and select **Check Out**.

3 Click **Check Out**.

Checking in a file to SharePoint

When you check in a file to SharePoint, other users are allowed to make changes to the file.

Shortcut	Tool Strip and Ribbon
Alt+F, H, I	File > SharePoint > Check In

To check in a file:

1 Select the file(s) you want to check in.

2 Select **File** > **SharePoint** > **Check In**.
—OR—
Right-click the file(s) and select **Check In**.

3 Click **Check In**.

Archive project

You can zip or export your project to archive it. Zipping a project is faster, but exporting a project allows you to specify which files are included in the archive.

Zipping a project

You can zip your project to archive it to a server or to send it to someone. When you zip a project in Flare, Flare creates an flprjzip file. Unlike a standard zip file, an flprjzip file can be emailed without the included JavaScript files being removed by an email filter.

Shortcut	Tool Strip and Ribbon
Alt+P, Z	Project > Zip Project

To zip a project:

1 Select **Project > Zip Project**.
   The Create Package dialog box appears.

2 Type or select a package file path and name.

3 Click **Create**.
   Flare creates the flprjzip file.

Exporting a project NEW!

You can export your project to archive all or selected files in a large project or to send selected files for translation.

Shortcut	Tool Strip and Ribbon
Alt+P, E, P	Project > Export Project

To export a project:

1 Select **Project** > **Export Project**.
The Export Project wizard appears.

2 Type a **New Project Name** for the exported project.

3 Type or select a **New Project Path** for the exported project.

4 For **Export From**, select whether you would like to export the entire project or only part of the project.

5 For Output, select whether you would like to create project files, a ZIP file, or a project template.

6 Click **Next**.

7 Select **Variables to text**.

8 Select **Convert snippets to text**.

9 Click **Finish**.

Sample questions for this section

1 Topic templates have the following extension:
A) htm
B) htt
C) temp
D) fltt

2 File tags can be applied to:
A) Topics only
B) Topics and images
C) Topics, images, videos, and sounds
D) Any type of file in your project

3 You can create reports based on the following information in Flare:
A) File tags
B) Used and unused styles, variables, and images
C) Both of the above
D) None of the above. You can only create reports in Analyzer.

4 Annotations and tracked changes are included when you send a topic for review in Contributor.
A) True
B) False

5 Reviewers need to install Flare to review your topics.
A) True
B) False

6 Flare provides built-in support for which source control applications?
A) Any that support the MS SCC API
B) Subversion (SVN) and CVS
C) VSS, TFS, SVN, and Perforce
D) All of them

7 Why would you use MadCap Pulse?

A) To send bug reports.

B) To send information to MadCap if Flare crashes.

C) To add surveys to your project.

D) To allow users to interact with each other and add comments to topics.

Accessibility

This section covers:

- [ ] Table headers, captions, and summaries
- [ ] Alt text for images, videos, and equations
- [ ] Access for WebHelp without stylesheets **NEW!**
- [ ] PDF Tagging
- [ ] Accessibility warnings

Accessibility overview

Accessibility focuses on making content accessible to all users, including users who may have challenges moving, seeing, and/or hearing. Accessibility features are recommended by Section 508 of the U.S Government's Rehabilitation Act and the W3C's Web Content Accessibility Guidelines (WCAG). Not providing accessible content is often seen as a form a discrimination, and many countries are introducing legislation to require accessibility features.

The following table lists the basic accessibility guidelines.

Accessibility guideline	See page
Include page titles	57
Use headings and table header rows	332
Include table captions and summaries	332
Include titles for links	334
Tag PDF documents	334
Include alt text for images	334
Include alt text for equations	335
Include alt text for videos	335
Support access when stylesheets are disabled	336
Specify the language for topics	340
Specify the language for blocks of content	341

Adding a header row to a table

You can add a header row to indicate how the content is organized in a table. Header rows also allow you to use a table style to format the header separately from normal table 'data' rows.

Shortcut	Tool Strip	Ribbon
Alt+B, O	Table > Table Properties	Table > Table Properties

To add a header row to a table:

1 Right-click inside a table and select **Table Properties**. The Table Properties dialog box appears.

2 Select the **General** tab.

3 For **Number of header rows**, select **1**.

4 Click **OK**.

Adding a caption and summary to a table

You can add table captions and summaries to increase accessibility. A table caption provides a literal description of the table, such as 'Monthly average temperatures in Bermuda.' A table summary provides a interpretation or summary of the table contents. For example, 'Bermuda's average monthly high temperatures are 68 to 86 degrees Fahrenheit, and the average low temperatures are 60 to 78 degrees Fahrenheit.

Shortcut	Tool Strip	Ribbon
Alt+B, O	Table > Table Properties	Table > Table Properties

To add a caption and summary to a table:

1 Right-click inside a table and select **Table Properties**. The Table Properties dialog box appears.

2 Select the **General** tab.

3 To add a caption:

☐ Type the caption **Text**.

☐ Select a **Side** for the caption.

☐ Select whether the caption should **Repeat** across printed pages.

☐ If the caption repeats, type the text to be appended to the caption on subsequent pages.
For example: **(cont)**

4   In the **Summary** text box, type a summary.

5   Click **OK**.

Adding a title to a link

The 'title' attribute to describe a link's destination. Screen readers read this information to help users decide if they want to click the link.

✎ *Flare refers to a link title as a "screen tip."*

Shortcut	Tool Strip	Ribbon
F4 or Crl+K	Insert > Hyperlink	Home > Properties

To add a title to a link:

1   Right-click a link and select **Edit Hyperlink**.
The Insert Hyperlink dialog box appears.

2   In the **Screen Tip** field, type a description of the link's destination.

3   Click **OK**.

Adding alt text to an image

You can add alt text to an image to provide a description for users who can't see the image.

Shortcut	Tool Strip	Ribbon
F4 or Ctrl+G	Insert > Image	Home > Properties

To add alt text to an image:

1   Right-click an image and select **Edit Image**.
The Edit Image dialog box appears.

2   Select the **General** tab.

3   In the **Alternate Text** field, type a description of the image.

4   If you want to use the same alt text for all images, select **Apply the alternate text and screen tip to all image references**.

5   Click **OK**.

Adding alt text to a video

You can add alt text to a video to provide a description for users who can't see the video.

Shortcut	Tool Strip	Ribbon
Alt+N, M	Insert > Multimedia	Home > Properties

To add alt text to a video:

1   Right-click an image and select **Edit Multimedia**. The Edit Image dialog box appears.

2   Select the **General** tab.

3   In the **Alternate Text** field, type a description of the video.

4   Click **OK**.

Adding alt text to an equation

You can add alt ('alternate') text to an equation to provide a description of the equation for a screen reader. For example, the equation $E=mc^2$ could use "E equals m c squared" as its alt text.

Shortcut	Tool Strip	Ribbon
Ctrl+E	Insert > Equation	Insert > Equation

To add alt text to an equation:

1   Right-click an equation and select **Edit Equation**. The Equation Editor appears.

2   In the **Alternate Text** field, type the text you want to add.

3 Click **OK**.

Automatically adding alt text NEW!

You can automatically add blank alt text to images, QR codes, and equations when you generate a target. Ideally, alt tags should describe the graphical element. However, this is a good option to use to meet accessibility requirements until you have time to write the alt text descriptions.

To automatically add blank alt text images, QR codes, and equations:

1 Open a target.

2 Select the **Advanced** tab.

3 Select **Use empty ALT text for images that do not have ALT text**.

Supporting access to WebHelp when stylesheets are disabled NEW!

Section 508 requires content to be accessible without a stylesheet. By default, the WebHelp and WebHelp Plus toolbar and navigation pane don't contain scrollbars. So, some of the content may not be visible, and there will be no way to view it if stylesheets are disabled. You can set your skin to add scrollbars when needed if the user is viewing your content without a stylesheet.

To add scrollbars when stylesheets are disabled:

1 Open a WebHelp skin.

2 Select the **Styles** tab.

3 Open the **Frame** style group.

4 Select the **Toolbar** style.

5 Open the **Frame** property group.

6 Set the **Scrolling** option to **auto**.

Tagging a PDF target

Tagging a PDF allows screen readers and other assistive technologies to identify headings, images, and tables, and other types of content in the document. The tags can then be used to determine the document's reading order and to provide navigational tools.

To tag a PDF target:

1 Open a PDF target.

2 Select the **PDF Options** tab.

3 Select **Generate tagged PDF**.

Finding and fixing accessibility issues

When you build any target, Flare can check your content for accessibility issues and provide a checklist to help you fix them.

To find and fix accessibility issues:

1 Open an online target.

2 Select the **Warnings** tab.

3 Select the accessibility issues you want to find and fix.

4 Build the target.

5 When the build is completed, click **Save Log**.
   The log is saved to the Reports folder.

6 Open the **Reports** folder.

7 Double-click the log report.

8 For each accessibility issue:

   □ Read the issue.

   □ Double-click the issue.
     The topic that contains the issue appears.

   □ Fix the issue.
     For example, add alternate text to an image.

9 Save the topic.

Additional resources

For more information about accessibility, see:

Wikipedia
en.wikipedia.org/wiki/Web_accessibility

US Government's Section 508 guidelines
www.section508.gov

W3C's Web Accessibility Initiative
www.w3.org/WAI

Internationalization

This section covers:

- Language settings for projects, topics, content blocks, skins, and targets
- Skin translation
- Project translation
- HTML Help localization

Selecting a language for a project

You can select a language for your project to specify the language to be used by the spell checker's dictionary.

Shortcut	Tool Strip	Ribbon
Alt+P, R	Project > Project Properties	Project > Project Properties

To select a language for a project:

1 Select **Project** > **Project Properties**.
The Project Properties dialog box appears.

2 Select the **Language** tab.

3 Select a language.

4 Click **OK**.

Selecting a language for a topic

You can select a language for a topic to specify the language to be used when spellchecking the topic. A topic's language setting is also used by screen readers and search engines to determine the topic's language.

Shortcut	Tool Strip	Ribbon
F4	Edit > Properties	Home > Properties

To select a language for a topic:

1 Right-click a topic and select **Properties**.
The Project Properties dialog box appears.

2 Select the **Language** tab.

3 Select a language.

4 Click **OK**.
A flag will appear at the top of your topic in the XML Editor to

indicate the language you selected. Users will not see the flag icon.

Selecting a language for a block of content

You can set the language for a block of content, such as a word, phrase, sentence or paragraph to specify the language to be used by the spell checker for the selected text.

Shortcut	Tool Strip	Ribbon
Alt+H, L, G	Format > Language	Home > Language

To select a language for a block of content:

1 Open a topic.

2 Highlight a block of content.

3 Select **Home** > **Language**.
The Language dialog box appears.

4 Select a language.

5 Click **OK**.
A flag will appear before the content in the XML Editor to indicate the language you selected. Users will not see the flag icon.

Translating a WebHelp skin

Flare provides translated versions of the default text used in WebHelp's labels and tool tips. You can modify the default text, or you can add a language skin for another language.

Shortcut	Tool Strip	Ribbon
Alt+T, M, L	Tools > Manage Language Skins	Tools > Manage Language Skins

To translate a WebHelp skin:

1 Select **Tools** > **Manage Language Skins**.
The Language Skins dialog box appears.

2 Select a language.

3 Click **Open File for Editing**.

4 If you selected a language in the list that is not boldfaced or does not have a path listed, select a language template for the new language skin and click **OK**.
The Language Skin Editor appears.

5 Select a style.

6 In the **General** group, select a **Label** or **Tooltip** value.

7 Type the translated label or tooltip.

TIP▶ *Language skins are stored in the C:\Users\admin\AppData\Roaming\MadCap Software\Flare\Language Skins folder. You can open and edit a language skin in a text editor if you are making numerous changes, or you can send the file to a translator.*

Translating an HTML5 skin

You can modify the default button and label text in an HTML5 skin or add your own translations.

To translate an HTML5 skin:

1 Open an HTML5 skin.

2 Select the **UI Text** tab.

3 Select a UI element.

4 Click the **Value** cell and type the translated text.

◇ *Changes to an HTML5 skin are stored in the skin instead of a language-specific file like WebHelp's language skins. If you are creating multiple HTML5 skins for a language, you will need to translate the text for each skin.*

Localizing your content

To localize a project, you (or a translator) will need to translate all of the content in your project. The recommended approach is to use MadCap Lingo to send the project to a translator. Lingo will automatically include all of the content that needs to be translated. If you try to collect and send the files yourself, it is extremely likely you forget to include some of the files, such as your glossary, auto-index phrase set, or TOC.

The translator can use Lingo or another application to translate the content. Lingo is integrated with Flare, so it is often the most efficient approach. However, other translation applications such as SDL Trados also work well with Flare projects.

Selecting a language for a target

You can select a language in a target to specify the language to use for the labels and tooltips in an online target. For WebHelp targets, the language setting specifies the WebHelp language skin to be used. For HTML5 targets, the language setting specifies the language option from the UI tab of the selected skin.

To select a language for a target:

1 Open a target.

2 Select the **Language** tab.

3 Select a language.

4 If you select a right-to-left language, make sure the right-to-left options are selected.

Building localized HTML Help

HTML Help does not provide full support for Unicode, so you may have problems building an HTML Help target that contains Cyrillic or double-byte characters or uses a right-to-left language. One potential fix is to change the system locale setting in Windows before building an HTML Help target, especially if your filenames contain Unicode characters.

To set the Windows system locale:

1 Open the Windows Control Panel.

2 Double-click **Region and Language.**

3 Select the **Administrative** tab.

4 Click **Change System Locale.**

5 Select a language.

6 Click **OK.**

7 Click **Restart Now.**

Flare customization

This section covers customizing Flare's:

- ☐ Interface
- ☐ Quick Access toolbar
- ☐ Pane layout options
- ☐ Window layout
- ☐ Analyzer data collection
- ☐ Auto suggestions

It also covers adding features to Flare using the plugin API.

Interface options

You can turn off Flare's ribbon if you prefer Flare 7 and earlier versions' toolbar-based interface.

To set the interface options:

1 Select **File** > **Flare Options**.
   The Options dialog box appears.

2 Select the **Interface** tab.

3 Select a **Menu Style**.
   If you select **Tool Strip**, Flare's UI will resemble Flare 7.

4 Select a **Theme**.

5 Click **OK**.

Quick Access toolbar options

You can add buttons to the Quick Access toolbar for common tasks. The Quick Access toolbar buttons can be accessed using Alt keyboard shortcuts. For example, the first button (Save) is Alt+1.

To add a button to the Quick Access toolbar:

1 Open the ribbon that contains the button you want to add.

2 Right-click the button and select **Add to Quick Access toolbar**.

To remove a button from the Quick Access toolbar:

☐ Right-click the button and select **Remove from Quick Access toolbar**.

To move the Quick Access toolbar above or below the ribbon:

☐ Right-click the Quick Access toolbar and select **Show Quick Access toolbar below the Ribbon**.

Pane layout options

By default, the left and right window panes organize windows using an accordion. You can change this setting to use tabs.

To use window tabs instead of an accordion:

1 Right-click inside the open pane's title bar.

2 Select **Standard Tabs (Top)** or **Standard Tabs (Bottom)**.

Moving windows

You can open, close, and rearrange Flare's windows or even open a topic or accordion item in a floating window. If you customize the interface, you can save the layout and switch between your layout or the default layout as needed.

To move a window:

1 Click inside the window.

2 Select **Window** > **Float**.

To reload the default layout:

1 Select **File** > **Reload Layout**.

2 Click **OK**.

To save the layout:

1 Select **File** > **Save Layout**.

2 Type a name for the layout.

3 Click **OK**.

To select a layout:

1 Select **File** > **Select Layout.**

2 Select a layout.

3 Click **OK.**

Analyzer options

You can turn off the Analyzer options to improve Flare's performance. However, it will take longer to generate Analyzer reports if the options are turned off.

To set the Analyzer options:

1 Select **File** > **Flare Options.**
The Options dialog box appears.

2 Select the **Analyzer** tab.

3 Select the **Advanced Scan** options.

4 If your project is very large, you can use the **Search Limits** option to reduce the number of search results in Analyzer reports.

5 Click **OK.**

Auto suggestion options

You can turn on the auto suggestion options to quickly select and insert frequently-used snippets, variables, or other content.

To set the auto suggestion options:

1 Select **File** > **Flare Options.**
The Options dialog box appears.

2 Select whether you want to enable auto suggestions.

3 If you enable auto suggestions:

☐ Select whether you want to enable snippet suggestions.

□ Select the max number of suggestions.

□ Select a minimum character length before the suggestions appear.

□ Select the variable sets, snippets, and/or suggestion term lists to be used to make suggestions.

4 Click **OK**.

To create an auto suggestion list:

1 Select **File** > **New**.
The Add File dialog box appears.

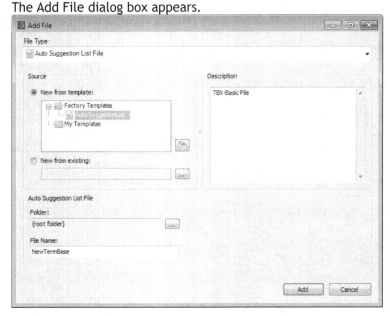

2 For **File Type**, select **Auto Suggestion List File**.

3 Select a **Source Template**.

4 Type a **File Name**.

5 Click **Add**.
The Copy to Project dialog box appears.

6 Click **OK**.

The Auto Suggestion File opens in the Auto Suggestion List Editor.

7 Click 📄.

8 Type a phrase.

Plug-in API

You can use the new plug-in API to customize or add menus, toolbars, buttons, and features to Flare.

To download the plug-in API, see www.madcapsoftware.com/downloads/redistributables.aspx

To integrate a DLL with Flare:

1 Close Flare.

2 In Windows, open the **Flare.app\Plugins** folder.

By default, the Plugins folder is in C:\Program Files (x86)\MadCap Software\MadCap Flare V10\Flare.app.

3 Paste your DLL into the Plugins folder.

4 Open Flare.

5 Select **File** > **Options**.

The Options dialog box appears.

6 Select the **Plugins** tab.

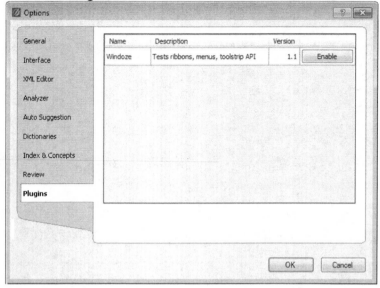

7 Click **Enable**.

8 Click **OK**.

9 Restart Flare.

Appendices

This section covers:

- ☐ Additional resources
- ☐ Keyboard shortcuts
- ☐ Guide to Flare files
- ☐ Quick task index
- ☐ Answers to sample questions

Additional resources

Reporting Flare bugs

MadCap does an excellent job of responding to customer problems and fixing bugs. To submit a bug report, select **Help** > **Report a bug**.

Requesting new features

MadCap encourages users to request new features. You can request a feature by selecting **Help** > **Report a bug** (feature requests use the same form as bug reports).

Crash reporting NEW!

If Flare crashes, a dialog box will appear that describes the problem. After you review the information, you can send a crash report to MadCap, view more details, or save the report to send to technical support later.

Flare discussion forums

You can use the Flare discussion forums to research Flare issues, post questions, and meet other Flare users. It's a very active and friendly community. You can visit the discussion groups by selecting **Help** > **Help Community** or by typing www.forums.madcapsoftware.com into a browser.

Keyboard shortcuts (by task)

Opening projects, files, and windows

Shortcut	Description
Alt+F4	Close Flare
Ctrl+F4	Close the current window
F4	Open the Properties dialog box from the Content Explorer
Ctrl+Shift+F8	Open the 'master' page layout
Ctrl+Shift+F9	Open the 'master' stylesheet
Ctrl+Shift+F12	Open a the Attributes window
Alt+B	Open the Table ribbon or menu
Alt+E	Open the Help ribbon or menu
Alt+H	Open the Home ribbon or menu
Alt+I	Open the Insert ribbon or menu
Alt+P	Open the Project ribbon or menu
Alt+R	Open the Review ribbon or menu
Alt+S	Open the Source Control ribbon or menu
Alt+T	Open the Tools ribbon or menu
Alt+V	Open the View ribbon or menu
Alt+W	Open the Window ribbon or menu
Ctrl+O	Open
Ctrl+T	Create a new file
Ctrl+Tab	Open a 'task switcher' popup displaying icons for all open windows. Press Ctrl+Tab again to move through the list.

Shortcut	Description
Ctrl+Shift+Tab	After pressing Ctrl+Tab, move backward through open window list.
Ctrl+Shift+P	Open the Properties dialog box from within the XML Editor

Selecting, moving, cutting, copying, and deleting content

Shortcut	Description
Alt+Shift+↑	Move the selected blocks of content up **NEW!**
Alt+Shift+↓	Move the selected blocks of content down **NEW!**
Ctrl+←	Move the cursor to the next word to the left
Ctrl+→	Move the cursor to the next word to the right
Ctrl+Shift+←	Select the next word to the left
Ctrl+Shift+→	Select the next word to the right
Ctrl+1	List matches (Auto Suggestion)
Ctrl+2	List frequent phrases (Auto Suggestion)
Ctrl+3	List variables (Auto Suggestion)
Ctrl+A	Select all
Ctrl+C	Copy
Ctrl+V	Paste
Ctrl+X	Cut

Shortcut	Description
Ctrl+Y	Redo
Ctrl+Z	Undo
Ctrl+Backspace	Delete text to the left until the next space
Ctrl+Delete	Delete text to the right to the next space
Ctrl+Insert	Copy
Shift+Delete	Cut
Shift+Insert	Paste
Shift+Tab	Select the previous cell in a table
Del	Delete
Tab	Select the next cell in a table, or when you press Tab in the last row of a table, add a new row
End	Move cursor to the end of the line
Shift+End	Select content between cursor and the end of the line

Formatting and tagging content

Shortcut	Description
F12	Open the Style window
Ctrl+F12	Open the Local Formatting window
Ctrl+Alt+B	Open the Paragraph (or Cell) Properties dialog box
Ctrl+Shift+B	Open the Font Properties dialog box
Ctrl+Shift+C	Open the Condition Tags dialog box

Shortcut	Description
Ctrl+Shift+H	Open the Style Picker
Shift+F12	Open the Attributes window
Ctrl+B	Bold
Ctrl+I	Italic
Ctrl+U	Underline

Inserting content

Shortcut	Description
F11	Insert quick character
Ctrl+;	Insert a paragraph in a list
Ctrl+E	Insert an equation
Ctrl+G	Insert a graphic
Ctrl+Q	Insert a QR code
Ctrl+R	Insert a snippet
Ctrl+Shift+V	Insert a variable
Shift+F11	Open the Character dialog box

Linking

Shortcut	Description
Ctrl+K	Insert a hyperlink
Ctrl+Shift+K	Insert a bookmark
Ctrl+Shift+R	Insert a cross reference

Shortcut	Description
Ctrl+Shift+T	Insert a glossary term link
Shift+F9	Open the Concepts window

Saving

Shortcut	Description
Ctrl+S	Save
Alt+Ctrl+S	Save as
Ctrl+Shift+S	Save all

Spell checking and tracking changes

Shortcut	Description
F7	Open the Spell Check window
Ctrl+Shift+E	Enable track changes

Working with the index and TOC

Shortcut	Description
F2	Highlight TOC entry for editing
F9	Open the Index window
F10	Insert the selected text as an index keyword

Ctrl+F8	Open the 'master' TOC

Searching

Shortcut	Description
F3	Find next
Ctrl+Shift+F	Open the Find and Replace in Files window **NEW!**
Ctrl+F	Open Quick Find widget **NEW!**
Ctrl+H	Open Quick Replace widget **NEW!**

Opening and docking windows

Shortcut	Description
Ctrl+[	Open the Project Organizer
Ctrl+J	Open the Content Explorer
Ctrl+W	Open the preview
Ctrl+Shift+D	Move the active document to the Document Dock
Ctrl+Shift+I	Open the Instant Messages window
Ctrl+Shift+J	Open the File List
Ctrl+Shift+O	Open the Messages window
Ctrl+Shift+W	Open the Start page

Opening Flare's help system

Shortcut	Description
F1	Open a context-sensitive help topic
Alt+Ctrl+F1	Open the help system's TOC
Alt+F1	Open the help system's index
Alt+Shift+F2	Open the help system's index results window
Ctrl+F1	Open the help system's search
Ctrl+F3	Open a context-sensitive help topic in the dynamic help window

Publishing

Shortcut	Description
F6	Build the primary target
Ctrl+F6	Publish the primary target
Ctrl+F9	Open the primary target in Target Editor
Shift+F6	Open the primary target

Keyboard shortcuts (by key)

Shortcut	Description
Alt+Ctrl+B	Open the Paragraph (or Cell) Properties dialog box
Alt+Ctrl+S	Save as
Alt+Ctrl+F1	Open the Flare help system's TOC
Alt+Shift+F2	Open the Flare help system's index results window
Alt+Shift+↑	Move the selected blocks of content up **NEW!**
Alt+Shift+↓	Move the selected blocks of content down **NEW!**
Alt+F1	Open the Flare help system's index
Alt+F4	Close Flare
Alt+1-9	Quick Access toolbar buttons
Alt+B	Open the Table ribbon or menu
Alt+E	Open the Help ribbon or menu
Alt+H	Open the Home ribbon or menu
Alt+N	Open the Insert ribbon or menu
Alt+P	Open the Project ribbon or menu
Alt+R	Open the Review ribbon or menu
Alt+S	Open the Source Control ribbon or menu
Alt+T	Open the Tools ribbon or menu
Alt+V	Open the View ribbon or menu
Alt+W	Open the Window ribbon or menu
Ctrl+F1	Open the Flare help system's search
Ctrl+F3	Open a context-sensitive help topic
Ctrl+F4	Close active window

Shortcut	Description
Ctrl+F6	Publish the primary target
Ctrl+F8	Open the 'master' TOC
Ctrl+F9	Open Primary target in Target Editor
Ctrl+F12	Open the Formatting window
Ctrl+1	List matches (Auto Suggestion)
Ctrl+2	List frequent phrases (Auto Suggestion)
Ctrl+3	List variables (Auto Suggestion)
Ctrl+A	Select all
Ctrl+B	Bold
Ctrl+C	Copy
Ctrl+E	Insert an equation
Ctrl+F	Open the Quick Find widget **NEW!**
Ctrl+G	Insert a graphic
Ctrl+H	Open the Quick Replace widget **NEW!**
Ctrl+I	Italic
Ctrl+J	Opens the Content Explorer
Ctrl+K	Insert a hyperlink
Ctrl+O	Open
Ctrl+P	Print
Ctrl+Q	Insert a QR code
Ctrl+R	Insert a snippet
Ctrl+S	Save
Ctrl+T	Create a new file
Ctrl+U	Underline
Ctrl+V	Paste
Ctrl+W	Open the preview
Ctrl+X	Cut

Shortcut	Description
Ctrl+Y	Redo
Ctrl+Z	Undo
Ctrl+[	Open the Project Organizer
Ctrl+;	Insert a paragraph in a list
Ctrl+Backspace	Delete text to the left until the next space
Ctrl+Delete	Delete text to the right to the next space
Ctrl+Insert	Copy
Ctrl+←	Move the insertion point to the next word to the left
Ctrl+→	Move the insertion point to the next word to the right
Ctrl+Shift+F8	Open the 'master' page layout
Ctrl+Shift+F9	Open the 'master' sylesheet
Ctrl+Shift+F12	Open the Attributes window
Ctrl+Shift+B	Open the Font Properties dialog box
Ctrl+Shift+C	Open the Condition Tags dialog box
Ctrl+Shift+D	Move the active document to the Document Dock
Ctrl+Shift+E	Enable track changes
Ctrl+Shift+F	Open the Find and Replace in Files window **NEW!**
Ctrl+Shift+H	Open the Style Picker
Ctrl+Shift+I	Open the Instant Messages window
Ctrl+Shift+J	Open the File List
Ctrl+Shift+K	Insert a bookmark
Ctrl+Shift+O	Open the Messages window
Ctrl+Shift+P	Open the Properties dialog box from within the XML Editor
Ctrl+Shift+R	Insert a cross reference
Ctrl+Shift+S	Save all
Ctrl+Shift+T	Insert a glossary term link
Ctrl+Shift+V	Insert a variable

Shortcut	Description
Ctrl+Shift+W	Open the Start page
Ctrl+Shift+←	Select the next word to the left
Ctrl+Shift+→	Select the next word to the right
Ctrl+Shift+Tab	After pressing Ctrl+Tab, move backward through open window list
Ctrl+Tab	Open a 'task switcher' popup. Press Ctrl+Tab to move through a list of open windows
Del	Delete
F1	Open a context-sensitive help topic
F2	Highlight for editing
F3	Find next
F4	Open the Properties dialog box from the Content Explorer
F5	Refresh
F6	Build the primary target
F7	Open the Spell Check window
F9	Open the Index window
F10	Insert the selected text as an index keyword
F11	Insert quick character
F12	Open the Style window
Shift+F6	Open the primary target
Shift+F9	Open the Concepts window
Shift+F11	Open the Character dialog box
Shift+F12	Open the Attributes window
Shift+Delete	Cut
Shift+End	Select content between cursor and the end of the line
Shift+Insert	Paste
Shift+Space	Insert non-breaking space

Shortcut	Description
Shift+Tab	Select the previous cell in a table
Tab	Select the next cell in a table, or, if you press Tab in the last row of a table, add a new row
End	Move cursor to the end of the line

Guide to Flare files

The following table lists all of the file types that are used in Flare, their extension, and their default folder.

File Type	Extension	Default Folder
Analyzer database	fldb	Analyzer\Content.cadbf
Auto suggestion list	fltbx	Project\Advanced
Batch target	flbat	Project\Targets
Browse sequence	flbrs	Project\Advanced
Condition tag set	flcts	Project\ConditionTagSets
Context-sensitive help alias file	flali	Project\Advanced
Context-sensitive help header file	h or hh	Project\Advanced
Contribution template	mccot	Documents\My Contribution Templates
Dependency set	fllnks	Output\Temporary
Dictionary (Sentry)	tlx	Program Files (x86)\MadCap Software\ MadCap Flare V10\Flare.app\Resources\ SSCE
Dictionary (Sentry, old format)	clx	Program Files (x86)\MadCap Software\ MadCap Flare V10\Flare.app\Resources\ SSCE
Dictionary (Hunspell)	oxt	Program Files (x86)\MadCap Software\ MadCap Flare V10\Flare.app\Resources\ HunspellDict
DITA topic	dita	Output\name of DITA target

File Type	Extension	Default Folder
DITA map	ditamap	Output\name of DITA target
DITA import template	flimpdita	Project\Imports
DotNet Help entry file	mchelp	Output\name of DotNet Help target
EPUB file	epub	Output\name of EPUB target
Flare ZIP file	flprjzip	Documents
FrameMaker import file	flimpfm	Project\Imports
Glossary	flglo	Project\Glossaries
HTML Help	chm	Output\name of HTML Help target
Image	bmp, emf, eps, exps, gif, hdp, jpg, png, ps, svg, tif, webm, wdp, wmf, xaml, xps	Content\Resources\Images
Index auto-index phrase set	flaix	Project\Advanced
Index link set	flixl	Project\Advanced
Language skin	fllng	Program Files (x86)\MadCap Software\ MadCap Flare V10\Flare.app\Resources\ LanguageSkins
Master page	flmsp	Content\Resources\MasterPages
Page layout	flpgl	Content\Resources\PageLayouts
PDF file	pdf	Output\name of PDF target
Project file	flprj	top-level folder
Project import file	flimpfl	Project\Imports
Publishing destination	fldes	Project\Destinations
Relationship	flrtb	Project\Advanced

File Type	Extension	Default Folder
table		
Report	flrep	Project\Reports
Review package	fltrev	Content
Search filter set	flsfs	Project\Advanced
Search synonyms	mcsyns	Project\Advanced
Skin	flskn	Project\Skins
Snippet	flsnp	Content\Resources\Snippets
Sound	mid, mpa, mp3, wav, wma	Content\Resources\Multimedia
Stylesheet	css	Content\Resources\Stylesheets
Table stylesheet	css	Content\Resources\TableStyles
Target	fltar	Project\Targets
Target build error log	mclog	Project\Reports
Template	htm	Documents\My Templates\Content
TOC	fltoc	Project\TOCs
Topic (generated)	htm	Output
Topic (source)	htm	Content
Variable set	flvar	Project\VariableSets
Video	mov, mpg, ogg, qt, swf, webm, wmv	Content\Resources\Multimedia
WebHelp AIR entry file	air	Output\name of WebHelp AIR target
Window layout	panellayout	Documents and Settings\ Application Data\MadCap Software

File Type	Extension	Default Folder
Word import file	flimp	Project\Imports
XHTML document	xhtml	Output\name of XHTML target
XPS document	xps	Output\name of XPS target

Quick task index

The quick task index provides the basic steps for every major task you can perform in Flare.

Concept	See Page
Projects	372
Topics	374
Topic content	376
Links	377
Navigational tools	381
Formatting	383
Variables and snippets	384
Condition tags	385
Targets	386
Context-sensitive help	390

Projects

Task	Steps	See Page
Creating a project	1 Select **File** > **New Project** > **New Project**. 2 Type a **Project Name** and **Project Folder**. 3 Select a **Language** and click **Next**. 4 Select a **Template Folder** and **Template** and click **Next**. 5 Select an **Available Target** and click **Finish**.	28
Importing a RoboHelp project	1 Select **File** > **New Project** > **RoboHelp Project**. 2 Select a project and click **Open**. 3 Click **Next**. 4 Type a **Project Name**, select a **Project Folder**, and click **Next**. 5 Select whether you want to **Convert all topics at once** and/or to **Convert inline formatting to CSS styles** and click **Next**. 6 Select a language for the spell checker and click **Finish**.	42
Importing an HTML Help file	1 Select **File** > **New Project** > **HTML Help Project (HHP)**. 2 Select a project, and click **Open**. 3 Click **Next**. 4 Type a **Project Name**, select a **Project Folder**, and click **Next**. 5 Select whether you want to **Convert all topics at once** and/or to **Convert inline formatting to CSS styles** and click **Next**. 6 Select a language for the spell checker and click **Finish**.	38
Creating a project based on a FrameMaker document	1 Select **File** > **New Project** > **FrameMaker Documents**. 2 Type a **Project Name** and type or select a **Project Folder**. 3 Select an **Output Type** and click **Next**. 4 Click ⊞, select an FM or book file, and click **Open**. 5 Select whether you want to link to the original	43

Task	Steps	See Page
	FrameMaker document and click **Next**.	
	6 Select a style or styles to use to create new topics and click **Next**.	
	7 Select how you want to import images and whether you want to import table styles.	
	8 Select whether you want to automatically reimport from FrameMaker whenever you build a target and click **Next**.	
	9 Select a stylesheet and click **Next**.	
	10 Map your styles and click **Finish**.	
Creating a project based on a Word document	1 Select **File > New Project > Word Documents**.	66
	2 Type a **Project Name** and type or select a **Project Folder**.	
	3 Select an **Output Type** and click **Next**.	
	4 Click ⊞, select a file, and click **Open**.	
	5 Select whether you want to link to the original Word document and click **Next**.	
	6 Select a style or styles to use to create new topics and click **Next**.	
	7 Select whether you want to automatically reimport from Word whenever you build a target.	
	8 Select how you want to import tables and headers/footers and click **Next**.	
	9 Select a stylesheet and click **Next**.	
	10 Map your styles and click **Finish**.	
Importing a DITA document set	1 Select **File > New Project > DITA Document Set**.	72
	2 Type a **Project Name** and type or select a **Project Folder**.	
	3 Select an **Output Type** and click **Next**.	
	4 Click ⊞, select a .dita or .ditamap file, and click **Open**.	
	5 If you plan to continue editing the original DITA files, select **Link generated files to source files**.	
	6 Click **Next**.	
	7 Type a **Project Name**.	

Task	Steps	See Page
	8 Type or select a **Project Folder** and click **Next.**	
	9 Select **Import all content files to one folder** if you want to import all of the DITA documents into one folder.	
	10 Select **'Auto-reimport before Generate Output'** if you want to automatically re-import the DITA document(s) when you generate a target.	
	11 Select **Preserve ID attributes for elements** if you plan to build a DITA target from your project.	
	12 Click **Next.**	
	13 Click **Conversion Styles** if you want to change the formatting of your topics.	
	14 Select a stylesheet for the new topic(s).	
	15 Click **Finish.**	

Topics

Task	Steps	See Page
Creating a topic	1 Select **File > New.**	55
	2 For **File Type**, select **Topic.**	
	3 Select a **Source** template.	
	4 Type a **File Name.**	
	5 Click **Add.**	
Importing a FrameMaker document	1 Create or open a FrameMaker import file.	42
	2 Click ⊞.	
	3 Select a FrameMaker FM or book document and click **Open.**	
	4 Select whether you want to link the generated files to the source files.	
	5 Select the **New Topic Styles** tab and select the styles to use to create new topics.	
	6 Select the **Options** tab and select how you want to import image and table styles.	
	7 Select the **Stylesheet** tab and select a	

Task	Steps	See Page
	stylesheet.	
	8 Select the **Paragraph Styles** tab and map your paragraph styles.	
	9 Select the **Character Styles** tab and map your character styles.	
	10 Select the **Cross Reference Styles** tab and map your cross-reference (x-ref) styles.	
	11 Click **Import** and click **Accept**.	
Importing a Word document	1 Create or open an MS Word import file.	66
	2 Click 🔲.	
	3 Select a Word document and click **Open**.	
	4 Select whether you want to link the generated files to the source files.	
	5 Select the **New Topic Styles** tab and select the styles to use to create new topics.	
	6 Select the **Options** tab and select how you want to import tables and headers/footers.	
	7 Select the **Stylesheet** tab and select a stylesheet.	
	8 Select the **Paragraph Styles** tab and map your paragraph styles.	
	9 Select the **Character Styles** tab and map your character styles.	
	10 Click **Import** and click **Accept**.	
Importing a DITA file	1 Create or open a DITA import file.	72
	2 Click 🔲.	
	3 Select a .dita or .ditamap file and click **Open**.	
	4 Select whether you want to link the generated files to the source files.	
	5 Select the **Options** tab and select whether you want to import your content into one folder.	
	6 Select the **Stylesheet** tab and select a stylesheet.	
	7 Click **Import** and click **Accept**.	
Importing an HTML file	1 Select **Project > Import HTML File Set**.	77
	2 Select **Import into this project**.	
	3 Click 🔲.	

Task	Steps	See Page
	4 Select a .htm, .html, or .xhtml document and click **Open**.	
	5 Select whether you want to link the generated files to the source files.	
	6 Click **Next**.	
	7 Select a folder for the imported topics.	
	8 Select **Import resources** if you also want to import any files that are used by the selected document(s).	
	9 Click **Finish**.	
Importing an external resource	1 Select **View > External Resources**.	79
	2 Click ⬛.	
	3 Select the folder that contains the external resource.	
	4 Click **OK**.	
	5 Select the file(s) you want to import.	
	6 Click ⬛.	
	7 Select a folder and click **OK**.	
Importing content from Flare projects	1 Create or open a Flare project import file.	77
	2 Click **Browse**.	
	3 Select a Flare project file and click **Open**.	
	4 Select whether you want to automatically re-import the files when you build a target.	
	5 For **Include Files**, select the files or file types to be linked.	
	6 For **Exclude Files**, select the file types to not be linked.	
	7 Click **Import**.	

Topic content

Task	Steps	See Page
Inserting a special character	1 Select **Insert > Character**.	60
	2 Select a character.	

Task	Steps	See Page
Inserting a QR code	1 Select **Insert > QR Code**. 2 Select a **Content Type**. 3 Type the **Content**. 4 Select a **Size**.	61
Inserting an equation	1 Select **Insert > Equation**. 2 Use the ribbons and toolbars to create the equation.	62
Creating a list	1 Click the down arrow to the right of the ⬚ button in the Home ribbon. 2 Select a list type. 3 Type the list items.	84
Sorting a list	1 Right-click the list's ol or ul tag. 2 Select **Sort List**.	85
Inserting an image	1 Select **Insert > Image**. 2 Click **Browse**, select an image, and click **Open**. 3 Type an **Alternate Text** description. 4 Click **OK**.	99
Inserting a sound or video	1 Select **Insert > Multimedia > *your movie type***. 2 Click **Browse**, select a sound or video file, and click **Open**. 3 Type an **Alternate Text** description.	101, 102

Tables

Task	Steps	See Page
Inserting a table	1 Select **Insert > Table**. 2 Select a number of columns and rows. 3 Select a number of header and footer rows. 4 Type a table caption and select a location. 5 Type a table summary. 6 Select a column width. 7 Click **OK**.	86

Task	Steps	See Page
Creating a table style	1 Select **File** > **New**. 2 For **File Type**, select **Table Style**. 3 Select a **Source** template. 4 Select a **Folder**. 5 Type a **File Name**. 6 Click **Add**.	88
Converting text to a table	1 Highlight the text. 2 Select **Insert** > **Table**. 3 In the **Text to Table** group box, select a conversion option. 4 Click **OK**.	88
Converting a table to text	1 Select the table. 2 Select **Table** > **Convert to Text**.	88
Sorting table rows	1 Click inside the column you want to use for sorting. 2 Select **Table** > **Sort Rows** > **Ascending** or **Descending**.	88
Rearranging table rows or columns	1 Select a row in the tag bar or a column in the span bar. 2 Drag the row up/down or the column left/right. 3 Release the mouse button to move the row or column.	89
Assigning a table style to a table	1 Click inside a table. 2 Click **Apply Table Style**. 3 Select a **Table Style**.	95
Assigning a table style to multiple tables	1 Open a table style. 2 Click **Apply Style**. 3 Select a topic or folder. 4 Click **OK**.	96
Removing inline formatting from a table	☐ Select **Table** > **Reset Local Cell Formatting**.	97

Links

Task	Steps		See Page
Creating a link	1	Select the text or image to use as the link.	112
	2	Select **Insert > Hyperlink.**	
	3	Select a link target (a topic, file, or website).	
	4	Select a **Target Frame.**	
	5	Type a **Screen Tip.**	
	6	Click **OK.**	
Creating an image map link	1	Right-click an image and select **Image Map.**	119
	2	Select an image map shape and draw the image map area.	
	3	Select a link target type and target.	
	4	Select a **Target Frame.**	
	5	Type a **Screen Tip.**	
	6	Click **OK.**	
Creating a topic popup	1	Select the text or image to use as the link.	121
	2	Select **Insert > Hyperlink > Topic Popup.**	
	3	Select a link target (a topic, file, or website).	
	4	Type a **Screen Tip.**	
	5	Click **OK.**	
Creating a text popup	1	Select the text or image that you want to use as the link.	123
	2	Select **Insert > Text Popup.**	
	3	Type the popup text.	
	4	Click **OK.**	
Creating a cross reference	1	Position your cursor where you want to add the cross reference.	124
	2	Select **Insert > Cross Reference.**	
	3	For **Link To**, select **Topic in Project.**	
	4	Select a topic and click **OK.**	
Finding and fixing broken links	1	Select **View > Project Analysis.**	120
	2	Select **Broken Links.**	
	3	Double-click a broken link in the list.	
	4	Right-click the highlighted link and select **Edit**	

Task	Steps	See Page
	Hyperlink.	
	5 Select a new link location.	
	6 Click **OK**.	

Drop-down, expanding, and toggler links

Task	Steps	See Page
Creating a drop-down link	1 Highlight the drop-down link and drop-down text.	126
	2 Select **Insert** > **Drop-Down Text**.	
	3 Highlight the drop-down link (or 'head').	
	4 Click **OK**.	
Creating an expanding link	1 Highlight the expanding link and expanding text.	127
	2 Select **Insert** > **Expanding Text**.	
	3 Highlight the expanding link (or 'hotspot').	
	4 Click **OK**.	
Creating a toggler link	1 Right-click the tag bar next to the content you want to show and hide.	128
	2 In the popup menu, select **Name**.	
	3 Type a name and click **OK**.	
	4 Highlight the toggler link text.	
	5 Select **Insert** > **Toggler**.	
	6 Select a toggler target.	
	7 Click **OK**.	

Related topic, keyword, and concept links

Task	Steps	See Page
Creating a related	1 Select **Insert** > **Related Topics Control**.	131
	2 Select a topic to add to the link.	

Task	Steps	See Page
topics link	3 Click ➡ to add the topic to the related topics link.	
	4 Add more topics as needed.	
	5 Click **OK**.	
Creating a keyword link	1 Select **Insert** > **Keyword Link Control**.	132
	2 Select a keyword.	
	3 Click ➡ to add the keyword to the keyword link.	
	4 Add more keywords as needed.	
	5 Click **OK**.	
Creating a concept link	1 Add a concept term to a topic or topics.	133
	2 Select **Insert** > **Concept Link**.	
	3 Select a concept.	
	4 Click ➡ to add the concept to the concept link.	
	5 Click **OK**.	

Relationship links

Task	Steps	See Page
Creating a relationship table	1 Select **File** > **New**.	136
	2 For **File Type**, select **Relationship Table**.	
	3 Select a **Template Folder** and **Template**.	
	4 Type a **File Name**.	
	5 Click **Add**.	
Adding a relationship to a relationship table	1 Open a relationship table.	137
	2 Click ▦ to create a new row.	
	3 Click ▤.	
	4 Type a name for the row.	
	5 Click **OK**.	
	6 Click a cell.	
	7 Click ▤.	
	8 Select a topic and click **OK**.	

Task	Steps	See Page
Creating a relationship link	1 Select **Insert > Proxy > Relationships Proxy.** 2 Click **OK.**	139

Navigational tools

Task	Steps	See Page
Creating a TOC book	1 Click 📕. 2 Press **F2.** 3 Type a name.	150
Creating a TOC page	1 Click 📄. 2 Double-click the TOC page. 3 Type a **Label** for the page. 4 Click **Select Link.** 5 Select a topic. 6 Click **Open.** 7 Click **OK.**	150
Finding and fixing issues in a TOC	1 If your TOC books are intentionally unlinked, click 📕. 2 Click 🔧. 3 Right-click the selected TOC item and select **Properties.** 4 On the **General** tab, select a new link and click **OK.**	151
Finding topics that are not in a TOC	1 Select **View > Project Analysis.** 2 Select **Topics Not In Selected TOC.** 3 For **Filter,** select a TOC.	156
Creating an index entry	1 Position the cursor where you want to insert the index entry marker. 2 Press **F9.** 3 Type the index entry and press **Enter.**	158

Task	Steps	See Page
Finding topics that are not in the index	1 Select **View > Project Analysis.** 2 Select **Topics Not In Index.**	165
Excluding a topic from the search	1 Right-click a topic and select **Properties.** 2 Select the **Topic Properties** tab. 3 Deselect the **Include topic when full-text search database is generated** option. 4 Click **OK.**	168
Creating a glossary entry and link	1 Highlight the word or phrase that will become the glossary link. 2 Select **Insert > Glossary Term Link.** 3 Select a **Glossary File.** 4 Type a definition. 5 Click **OK.**	172
Creating a browse sequence	1 Select **File > New.** 2 For **File Type,** select **Browse Sequence.** 3 Select a **Source** template. 4 Type a **File Name.** 5 Click **Add.**	176

Formatting and design

Task	Steps	See Page
Creating a stylesheet	1 Select **File > New.** 2 For **File Type,** select **Stylesheet.** 3 Select a **Source** template. 4 Type a **File Name.** 5 Click **Add.**	188
Creating a style	1 Use the **Home** ribbon commands to format the content. 2 Select the formatted content. 3 Select **Home > Style Window.**	191

Task	Steps	See Page
	4 Click **Create Style.**	
	5 Type a name for the new style.	
	6 Select whether the style should be applied to the highlighted content.	
	7 Click **OK.**	
Creating a master page	1 Select **File** > **New.**	206
	2 For **File Type**, select **Master Page.**	
	3 Select a **Source** template.	
	4 Type a **File Name.**	
	5 Click **Add.**	
Creating a page layout	1 Select **File** > **New.**	210
	2 For **File Type**, select **Page Layout.**	
	3 Select a **Source** template.	
	4 Type a **File Name.**	
	5 Click **Add.**	
Creating a skin	1 Select **File** > **New.**	218
	2 For **File Type**, select **Skin.**	
	3 Select a **Source** template.	
	4 Type a **File Name.**	
	5 Click **Add.**	
	6 Modify the skin options as needed.	

Variables and snippets

Task	Steps	See Page
Creating a variable	1 Click 📄 in the Variable Set Editor toolbar.	236
	2 Type a name for the variable.	
	3 Type a definition for the variable.	
Inserting a date/time variable	1 Click 📄 in the Variable Set Editor toolbar.	237
	2 Type a name for the variable.	
	3 Type a date and time format and click **OK.**	

Task	Steps	See Page
Inserting a variable	1 Select **Insert** > **Variable**. 2 Select a variable set. 3 Select a variable. 4 Click **OK**.	237
Creating a snippet from existing content	1 Highlight the content you want to convert to a snippet. 2 Select **Home** > **Create Snippet**. 3 Type a name for the snippet. 4 Select **Replace Source Content with the New Snippet**. 5 Click **Create**.	240
Creating a snippet from new content	1 Select **File** > **New**. 2 For **File Type**, select **Snippet**. 3 Select a **Source** template. 4 Type a **File Name**. 5 Click **Add**.	241
Inserting a snippet	1 Select **Insert** > **Snippet**. 2 Select a snippet. 3 Click **OK**.	242

Condition tags

Task	Steps	See Page
Creating a condition tag	1 Open a condition tag set. 2 Click 🗒 in the Condition Tag Set Editor toolbar. 3 Type a new name for the tag and press **Enter**. 4 Select a color.	244
Applying a condition tag to content	1 Select the content to be tagged. 2 Select **Home** > **Conditions**. 3 Select a condition tag's checkbox. 4 Click **OK**.	245

Task	Steps	See Page
Applying a condition tag to a topic, file, or folder	1 Select the topic, file, or folder to be tagged. 2 Click 🖳 in the Content Explorer toolbar. 3 Select the **Conditional Text** tab. 4 Select a condition tag's checkbox. 5 Click **OK**.	245
Applying a condition tag to a TOC book or page	1 Open the TOC. 2 Select a book or page and click 🖳. 3 Select the **Conditional Text** tab. 4 Select a condition tag's checkbox. 5 Click **OK**.	246

Targets

Task	Steps	See Page
Creating a target	1 Select **File > New**. 2 For **File Type**, select **Target**. 3 Select a **Source** template. 4 Type a **File Name**. 5 Click **Add**.	260
Building a target	☐ Right-click a target and select **Build**.	267
Viewing a target	☐ Right-click a target and select **View**.	269
Creating a publishing destination	1 Select **File > New**. 2 For **File Type**, select **Destination**. 3 Select a **Source** template. 4 Type a **File Name**. 5 Click **Add**.	272
Publishing a target	1 Open a target. 2 Click 🍇 Publish. 3 Select one (or more) of the publishing destinations.	272

Task	Steps	See Page
	4 Click **Start Publishing**.	
Batch generating targets	1 Create and open a batch target. 2 Select the **Schedule** tab. 3 Click **New**. 4 Select a frequency **Setting**. 5 Select a **Start** date and time. 6 If you selected a daily, weekly, or monthly frequency setting, select the recurrence details. 7 If the batch generate should repeat, select **Repeat task every** and specify how often and how long the repeating should occur. 8 If the repeating should expire, select **Expire** and specify an expiration date. 9 If you are ready to enable the batch generate, select **Enable**. 10 Click **OK**.	269

Context-sensitive help

Task	Steps	See Page
Creating a header file	1 Select **File > New**. 2 For **File Type**, select **Header File**. 3 Select a **Source** template. 4 Type a **File Name**. 5 Click **Add**.	277
Creating an alias file	1 Select **File > New**. 2 For **File Type**, select **Alias File**. 3 Select a **Source** template. 4 Type a **File Name**. 5 Click **Add**.	277
Assigning an identifier to a topic	1 Open an alias file. 2 Select an **Identifier**.	278

Task	Steps	See Page
	3 Select a **Topic**.	
	4 Click 📷.	
Testing context-sensitive help	1 Build your target. 2 Right-click the target in the Targets folder and select **Test CSH API Calls**. 3 Next to each identifier, click **Test**.	279

Templates

Task	Steps	See Page
Creating a topic template	1 Open the topic that will become the template. 2 Add and format the content you want to include in the template. 3 Select **File** > **Save** > **Save as Template**. 4 Type a **Template Name** and click **OK**.	284
Creating a Contribution template	1 Open the topic that will become the template. 2 Add and format the content you want to include in the template. 3 Select **File** > **Save** > **Save as Contribution Template**. 4 Type a **Template Name**. 5 Select a template location and click **Next**. 6 Select any content files the template uses and click **Next**. 7 Select any condition tags or variable sets the template uses and click **Next**. 8 Click **Finish**.	285

File tags and reports

Task	Steps	See Page
Creating a file tag set	1 Select **File** > **New**. 2 For **File Type**, select **File Tag Set**. 3 Select a **Source** template. 4 Type a **File Name**. 5 Click **Add**.	294
Adding a tag	1 Open a file tag set. 2 Click 📄. 3 Type a name for the tag.	295
Applying a tag	1 Right-click a file and select **Properties**. 2 Select the **File Tag** tab. 3 Select a **Tag Type**. 4 Select a **File Tag**. 5 Click **OK**.	295
Creating a report	1 Select **File** > **New**. 2 For **File Type**, select **Report File**. 3 Select a **Source** template. 4 Type a **File Name**. 5 Click **Add**.	298
Generating a report	1 Open a report. 2 On the **General** tab, type a **Title** for the report. 3 Select the **Tables** to include in the report. 4 Click **Generate**.	299

Annotation and topic reviews

Task	Steps	See Page
Adding an annotation	1 Position your cursor where you want to add the annotation. 2 Select **Review** > **Insert Annotation**.	302

Task	Steps	See Page
	3 If this is your first annotation, type your initials. 4 Type your annotation.	
Locking content	1 Position your cursor inside the content you want to lock. 2 Select **Review** > **Lock**.	303
Sending a topic for review	1 Select **Review** > **Send for Review**. 2 Type a **Review Package Name**. 3 Click , select the topics you want to send for review, and click **Open**. 4 Click **Next**. 5 Type a subject and message for the email. 6 Select a recipient. 7 Click **Send**.	303
Accepting a reviewed topic	1 Select **Review** > **Topic Reviews**. 2 Select **Inbox**. 3 Select a topic. 4 Click . 5 Click **OK**.	305

Pulse

Task	Steps	See Page
Enabling in a skin	1 Open a skin. 2 Select the **General** tab. 3 Select the **Community** option. 4 Select the **Community** tab. 5 Select **Display topic comments at the end of each topic**. 6 Select **Display Community Search Results**.	308
Enabling in a target	1 Open a target. 2 Select the **Community** tab.	309

Task	Steps	See Page
	3 Select **Enable Pulse/Feedback Server.**	
	4 Type your Pulse server's **URL.**	
	5 Click **Login.**	
	6 Type your **User name.**	
	7 Type your **Password.**	
	8 Click **OK.**	
	9 In the **Communities** field, select your Pulse community.	
Creating a profile	1 Open a WebHelp or HTML5 target in a browser.	310
	2 Select the **Community** tab or open a topic.	
	3 Click **Login.**	
	4 Click **Register.**	
	5 Type your **First Name** and **Last Name.**	
	6 Type your **Email Address.**	
	7 Type and confirm your **Password.**	
	8 Click **Register.**	
	9 Open your email and complete the registration.	
Editing a profile	1 Open a WebHelp or HTML5 target in a browser.	311
	2 Select the **Community** tab.	
	3 Click **Edit My Profile.**	
Viewing notifications	1 Open a WebHelp or HTML5 target in a browser.	311
	2 Select the **Community** tab.	
	3 Click **Notifications.**	
Viewing reports	1 Open your Pulse Admin site in a browser.	311
	2 Click **Administration.**	
	3 Select **Reports.**	
	4 Click a report.	

Source control

Task	Steps	See Page
Binding a project	1 Select **Project > Project Properties.**	313

Task	Steps	See Page
	2 Select the **Source Control** tab.	
	3 Click **Bind Project**.	
	4 Select a **Source Control Provider** and provide the required information.	
	5 Select **Keep files checked out** if you want to keep the files checked out after they are added to the source control application.	
	6 Click **OK**.	
Adding a file	1 Right-click a file or folder and select **Source Control > Add File**.	315
	2 If you want to keep editing the file, select **Keep Checked Out**.	
	3 Click **OK**.	
Getting the latest version	1 Right-click a file or folder and select **Source Control > Get Latest Version**.	316
	2 Click **OK**. If the files are different, click **Merge All** or **Resolve**.	
	3 Click **OK**.	
Checking out a file	1 Right-click a file or folder and select **Source Control > Check Out**.	316
	2 If you want to prevent other users from checking out the file, select **Lock Files**.	
	3 Click **Check Out**.	
Checking in a file	1 Right-click a file or folder and select **Source Control > Check In**.	317
	2 Type a check in **Comment**.	
	3 Select **Keep Checked Out** if you want to check in the current version and keep editing the file.	
	4 Click **Check In**.	
Viewing a list of checked out files	1 Select **Source Control > Pending Check-Ins**.	318
	2 Scroll to the right to view the Status and User columns.	
Viewing differences	1 Right-click a file and select **Source Control > View History**.	319
	2 Select two versions of the file.	
	3 Click **Show Differences**.	

Task	Steps	See Page
Rolling back	1 Right-click a file and select **Source Control** > **View History**. 2 Select a version of the file. 3 Click **Get Selected Version.**	319
Merging changes	1 Check in or get the latest version of a file. 2 Click **Auto Merge All.** 3 Click **OK.** 4 Click **Resolve.** 5 Select a resolution option.	320

Answers

Projects

		Answers
1	D	Flare projects have a .flprj ('Flare project') extension.
2	A	Flare does support Unicode.
3	D	You can create topics, stylesheets, and snippets based on a template.
4	B	You should select 'Link generated files to source files' if you want to keep editing an imported document in Word or FrameMaker.
5	D	When you import a RoboHelp project, only the skin's name is imported. You will need to set it up in Flare.
6	A	You can import FrameMaker .fm and .book files into Flare.
7	D	Styles, index keywords, and master pages are imported into Flare.

Topics

1	C	XHTML is an XML schema.
2	D	You can have as many topics open as you want.
3	D	You can link any Flare file between projects, including topics, stylesheets, page layouts, and variables.
4	B	To import a PDF file, you should save it as an HTML and import the HTML file.
5	C	Table styles are table-specific stylesheets, and they have a CSS extension.
6	D	You cannot insert ai files into Flare topics.
7	B	To view a list of topics that contain an image, right-click the image in the Content Explorer and select View Links.

Links

Navigation

1	C	TOC files are stored in the Project Organizer's TOCs folder.
2	A	TOC pages do not have to be inside books.
3	C	You can add second-level index entries using a colon.
4	D	You can select View > Index Window to view your index keywords. Index keywords are stored in your topics, not in an index file.
5	B	To exclude a topic from the search, open the Topic Properties dialog box and deselect the Include topic when full-text search database is generated option.
6	C	In HTML Help, the glossary appears at the bottom of your table of contents. It appears as an accordion in WebHelp.
7	B	A browse sequence is an ordered list of links that can be used to find and open topics, like a TOC.

Format and design

1   B   Inline formatting is applied by highlighting content and changing its appearance.

2   C   You should consider using a font set for WebHelp if your users are using different operating systems.

3   D   A master stylesheet is assigned to all topics.

4   A   The breadcrumb is the path to the current topic using the TOC.

5   D   You can create odd and even pages in a page layout to specify different footers in a print target.

6   C   The additional items will appear as icons below the accordion.

7   B   To select a skin, open the target and select the skin in the General tab.

Single source

1	A	Variables are stored in variable sets in the Project Organizer.
2	B and C	A variable's definition can be set in the VariableSet Editor and in a target on the Variables tab.
3	all	Snippets can contain formatted text, tables, lists, and variables.
4	C	Snippets are stored in snippet files in the Content Explorer.
5	all	Condition tags can be applied to topics, folders, TOC books and pages, and index keywords.
6	A	Flare automatically updates the content to use the new condition tag name.
7	all	Condition tags can be used with any target type.

Build and publish

1	A and C	MadCap Software created the DotNet Help and WebHelp formats. The HTML Help and XPS formats were created by Microsoft.
2	C	The 'Insert Mark of the Web' option will turn off the 'Active Content' message when you open WebHelp locally from your PC.
3	D	A primary target is the target you plan to create the most often. It also sets the target that is used for the preview. However, you can create any target type from your project.
4	D	You can set up as many targets as you need for your project.
5	C	Flare deletes everything in the Output folder when you select Build > Clean project.
6	B	Flare copies your files to a network or website when you publish a target.
7	B	The 'startup' topic is the first topic users see when they open an online target.

Project management

1	A	Topic templates use the same extension as topics: htm.
2	D	File tags can be applied to any type of file, including topics, images, videos, sounds, master pages, page layouts, skins, and stylesheets.
3	C	You can create reports based on file tags and/or unused or used styles, variables, and images.
4	A	Annotations and tracked changes are included when you send a topic for review in Contributor.
5	B	Reviewers can use Contributor to review topics. They do not need to install Flare.
6	C	Flare provides built-in support for VSS, TFS, SVN, and Perforce.
7	D	Pulse can be used to allow users to interact with each other and add comments to topics.

Index

CSS to the Point

CSS to the Point provides focused answers to over 150 cascading stylesheet (CSS) questions. Each answer includes a description of the solution, a graphical example, and sample code that has been tested in Internet Explorer, Firefox, Opera and Safari. If you have been struggling with CSS, this book will help you use CSS like a pro.

You can order *CSS to the Point* at **www.lulu.com/clickstart**.

HTML5 to the Point

HTML5 to the Point provides focused answers to over 140 HTML5 questions. Each answer includes a description of the solution and sample code that you can use in your documents. If you want to learn HTML5, this book will help you use it like a pro.

You can order *HTML5 to the Point* at **www.lulu.com/clickstart**.

Word 2013 to the Point

Word 2013 to the Point provides answers to over 400 Microsoft Word questions. Each answer includes a description of the solution and step-by-step instructions. The invaluable tips and tricks will help you get started fast, and he comprehensive list of keyboard shortcuts will help you use Word 2013 like a pro.

You can order *Word 2013 to the Point* at **www.lulu.com/clickstart**.

Training

ClickStart offers training for Flare, Captivate, HTML5, and CSS. Our training classes extend what you have learned in this book with practice exercises, best practices, and advanced challenges.

We teach online and onsite classes (worldwide), and we offer group discounts for 4 or more students. For more information, visit our website at **www.clickstart.net** or email us at **info@clickstart.net**.

Consulting

Click**Start** also offers a full range of consulting and contracting services, including:

- ☐ Migrating RoboHelp, FrameMaker, and Word projects to Flare

- ☐ Developing best practices for creating online help, user guides, and policies and procedures

- ☐ Single sourcing content for multiple audiences

- ☐ Designing stylesheets, page layouts, master pages, skins, and style guides

- ☐ Developing context-sensitive help and embedded user assistance

For more information, visit our website at **www.clickstart.net** or email us at **info@clickstart.net**.